Information Literacy

INFORMATION LITERACY

What Does It Look Like in the School Library Media Center?

Ann Marlow Riedling

LIBRARIES
U N L I M I T E D
A Member of the Greenwood Publishing Group

Westport, Connecticut • London

Library of Congress Cataloging-in-Publication Data

Riedling, Ann Marlow, 1952–
    Information literacy : what does it look like in the school library media center? / by
Ann Marlow Riedling.
      p. cm.
    Includes bibliographical references and index.
    ISBN 1–59158–201–6 (pbk. : alk. paper)
    1. Information literacy—Study and teaching. 2. Information retrieval—Study and
teaching. 3. Library orientation for school children. 4. Media programs (Education).
5. School librarian participation in curriculum planning. I. Title.
ZA3075.R537   2004
025.5′678—dc22   2004048773

British Library Cataloguing in Publication Data is available.

Library of Congress Catalog Card Number: 2004048773
ISBN: 1–59158–201–6

First published in 2004

Libraries Unlimited, 88 Post Road West, Westport, CT 06881
A Member of the Greenwood Publishing Group, Inc.
www.lu.com

Printed in the United States of America

The paper used in this book complies with the
Permanent Paper Standard issued by the National
Information Standards Organization (Z39.48–1984).

10 9 8 7 6 5 4 3 2 1

Copyright Acknowledgment
Excerpts from *Information Power: Building Partnerships for Learning* by American Association of School Librarians for Educational Communications and Technology. Copyright ©
1998 American Library Association and Association for Educational Communications
and Technology. Reprinted by permission of the American Library Association.

Contents

Acknowledgments

When I write a book, I put all of my heart and soul into it. I honestly believe in school library media programs and information literacy. I *know* that they are of utmost importance in a school...and a community—actually, for the well-being of our world. In the midst of the twenty-first century, what is more important than information—and using it effectively and efficiently?

This book would not have been possible without Sharon Coatney, my editor. Not only is she unbelievably talented, but also a wonderful person and friend. Thank you.

I dedicate this textbook to all of the gifted school library media specialists that graduated from Spalding University, Louisville, Kentucky. I have never, ever been more proud of students—thank you!

Ann

Preface

What Does Information Literacy Look Like in the School Library Media Center? is designed for courses that prepare college and university students for undergraduate or graduate degrees in school library media. It is also written as a helpful instructional manual for practicing school library media specialists. The overall goal of this textbook is to teach library media specialists what information literacy looks like—in general, in the school, in the classroom, in your mind, in life and in motion.

Numerous textbooks have been written concerning a wide variety of aspects regarding information literacy. These books typically focus on one or two facets of information literacy (such as problem solving models, copyright, etc.) or are aimed at a specific audience (such as high school students or teachers). This textbook differs in that it is an all-inclusive, practical guidebook that discusses information literacy, research, independent learning, ethics, and more. It is aimed specifically for school library media specialists' use. In addition, this text includes helpful scenarios to explain or help picture "what it looks like." Current related readings and Web sites are also provided within each chapter so the school library media specialist can further explore information literacy.

An ongoing debate continues about who should teach information literacy skills. It is my belief that this should be a joint effort between the school library media specialist and the teacher. However, this does not always happen. Too often teachers send students to a library media center to conduct research without properly preparing them with the essentials of information literacy and the research process. In addition, library media specialists are challenged to teach information literacy skills with constantly changing tools. Therefore, this book is designed as a practical guide that leads school library media specialists through the information literacy procedure, such that they can effectively and knowledgeably relay this process to students of all ages. Becoming information literate—knowing how to learn—involves a drastic change from the way many students were accustomed to learning—and teachers were accustomed to teaching. School library media specialists *need* to know "what it looks like" from every viewpoint. Information literacy skills are imperative in today's world.

1

In General

INTRODUCTION

No other change in our nation has offered greater challenges than the emergence of the Information Age. In an information society, all people should have the right to access information that can enhance their lives. To reap the benefits of our global society, students must be information literate on a technological, global basis.

Our evolving world includes an incredible growth of knowledge, an explosion of technology, and a speedy reconfiguration of the boundaries that separate the myriad of academic fields and social conventions. This complex, global society continues to expand at a rate beyond the capacity of individuals to comprehend. Collectively, and with the use of technologies that have potentiated the momentum of change, humanity generates enormous amounts of information. Access to information is critical to ease the burden of change and to help humanity navigate its course toward the future. The abilities to access, comprehend, and use information have become the skills students must develop to function in our current world, as well as in the future.

Chapter 1 addresses the who, what, when, where, why, and how of information literacy. You will learn who needs to be information literate—and who needs to teach them; precisely what information literacy is all about (including definitions); when information literacy should be taught and learned; why being an information literate, lifelong learner is critical in today's society; and how information literacy is taught and learned (a brief introduction—the remaining chapters explain this in more detail). Information literacy covers many, many issues. As a school library media specialist, you should be more alert to these issues than anyone else in the school. You must become a leader— a leader with a vision and a plan.

A Closer Look

Information literacy forms the basis for lifelong learning. It is common to all disciplines, to all learning environments, and to all levels of education. It enables learners to master content and extend their investigations, become more self-directed, and assume greater control over their own learning. Students must learn to know when they need information, be able to locate information efficiently and effectively, evaluate information from a variety of sources, process the information gained, and use that information to make appropriate decisions. You, as a school library media specialist, are in a prime position to foster information literacy skills in students and teachers.

The amount of new information produced over the past few decades is nothing short of phenomenal. "Over three billion web pages are available on the World Wide Web and the number is growing by five million new pages a day" (Kranich, 2000, p. 7). Those two facts alone demonstrate the need for students to become information literate. What precisely is information literacy? Numerous individuals and organizations have developed meanings for information literacy. According to the American Library Association (ALA) (1989), information literacy is a set of abilities requiring individuals to recognize when information is needed and to have the ability to locate, evaluate, and effectively use the information needed. Whether information comes from a Web site, an online database, a magazine, a book, a government organization, a video, a conversation, a painting, or any number of possible sources, inherent in the concept of information literacy is the ability to dissect and understand what you see on the page or monitor, in posters, pictures, and other images, as well as what you hear. The American Association of School Librarians (AASL) (1998) states, "Information literacy—the ability to find and use information—is the keystone of lifelong learning. Creating a foundation for lifelong learning is at the heart of the school library media program" (p. 1).

To understand information literacy more thoroughly, you, as the school library media specialist, should become familiar with key terms that relate to information literacy:

Collaboration: To work jointly with others, especially in an intellectual endeavor.

Critical thinking skills: Higher-level thinking skills that include analysis and synthesis of ideas.

Independent learning: Learning information without the assistance of others.

Information literacy standards: Guidelines provided in Information Power: Building Partnerships for Learning *(AASL & Association for Educational and Communications Technology [AECT], 1998), which identify skills, behaviors, and attitudes students need to become information literate—independent, lifelong learners.*

Internet: An international network of computer networks.

Keyword searching: In keyword searching, the database software searches for the occurrence of the search term in one or more fields of each record, for example, in the title, abstract and descriptor fields.

Lifelong learners: People who know how to learn without assistance. This applies to all individuals, not merely students, over the span of their lives.

Plagiarism: To steal and pass off the ideas or words of another as one's own.

Problem-solving/problem-solving models: Basic steps in a research process.

Resource-based learning: Learning that results from the use of multiple resources in addition to, or other than, a traditional textbook.

World Wide Web: A system for making connections to other computers all over the world via hypertext links.

Our schools, school library media centers, and homes are filled with electronic technologies, but are we preparing our students and teachers for the bombardment of information that is provided by these technologies? What happens when a student can get more information from the Internet than previously conveyed by a teacher or print material? What should a student do when faced with so many information possibilities? Which of the information sources is credible and which is not? With so much more information (and *mis*information), students must not only have reading and computer skills, but information literacy skills as well. As explained by McGovern (2001), "Before our very eyes, witness the emergence of the information literate. The world is at their feet. The future is in their hands. Their hands are at the keyboard, and their eyes are on the screen. It is they who are shifting the present and shaping the future. The Internet is their tool of choice" (p. 16). Students who are information literate know how to use resources made available through any means to locate needed information. They understand the purposes, strengths, differences, and similarities of each provider and how they complement each other. An information literate student is able to use information resources effectively at each stage of a project, from defining a topic to critically evaluating the information found. Information literacy goes beyond merely having access to and knowledge of how to use technology. Technology alone does not guarantee quality learning experiences. As a school library media specialist, you must provide the expertise and leadership to help students become information literate. Who better than *you?*

To develop students who are information literate, school library media specialists, in collaboration with teachers and other school personnel, need to integrate information literacy skills *across the curriculum* in all subject areas, beginning at the earliest grades. The impact of moving from textbook-based learning to resource-based learning will involve greater use of library materials and a demand for more varied media resources, including print, nonprint, and Web-based. As a school library media specialist, you will need to frequently collaborate with teachers to provide training and guidance toward the sharpening of information literacy skills. And if you are not called on, it is imperative that you take the initiative! Developing information literate students will involve a drastic change from the way many are accustomed to learning. To become information literate will require students to know more and learn more about the world around them. It will compel students to be more self-directed and prepare them for real-life problem-solving and critical thinking skills. Students must be discerning learners, and they must be constantly learning. The overall goal is to prepare students to learn how to learn and to carry these skills into other areas of their lives so that they can be socially responsible, independent seekers and consumers of information throughout their lives. Information literacy is an active process that requires seeking out knowledge from multiple sources rather than passively receiving and repeating facts. Information literacy requires a deeper understanding of how and where to locate information, the ability to judge whether that information is meaningful, and ultimately, how best that information can be incorporated to address the problems and issues at hand. The responsibility for assisting students to achieve information literacy skills resides with the school library media specialist, teachers, administrators, and the school community. The school library media specialist, working collaboratively with these people, is *vital* to student learning—independent and lifelong.

Why, specifically, do students need to become information literate? Information literate students are

Competent
Independent
Socially responsible
Lifelong learners

Information literate students also know their information needs and actively engage in the world of ideas. Information literate students display confidence in their abilities to solve problems and know how to locate relevant and accurate information. They manage technology tools to access information and to communicate. Students who are information literate operate comfortably in situations where there are multiple answers; they are flexible and can adapt to change. Information literate students are capable of functioning independently and in groups. It is important, as a school library media specialist, to recognize when information literacy skills have been learned. When teaching information literacy skills, realize that

Knowledge seeking is a process.
Quality products are necessary in *all* content areas.
Self-directed learning skills are critical in developing lifelong, independent learners.

The school library media center is where individual differences mesh with the diversity of resources and technology available. Responsible students make ethical information decisions.

Information literate students (at the "advanced level")

Can determine information needs
Recognize and understand the value of information
Develop information-seeking strategies and locate information efficiently
Are inquisitive and always willing to learn
Are able to isolate where new information is required to solve a problem
Respect the principle of intellectual freedom
Understand the ethical, legal, and socioeconomic issues surrounding information and information technology
Are able to follow guidelines and etiquette using electronic information sources
Can evaluate content critically and competently
Can revise and refine, as well as reflect information
Have the ability to use content accurately and creatively
Can manage, analyze, critique, and cross-reference information into usable knowledge
Are able to create quality content
Are independent-minded, but realize that collaboration is the best way to acquire and develop knowledge
Have the ability to communicate what they know in an effective manner
Realize that information does not become knowledge until contemplated by the mind

Good decisions depend on good information. Good decision makers are information smart. They know how to locate, evaluate, organize, and use information. They have also learned how to separate the true from the untrue and realize that real information power is having the right information *when they need it.* In our information-rich society, school library media specialists must also be information smart. School library media specialists *are* the ultimate search engines! You can help students and teachers save time and money by assisting them to locate the best, most current, and appropriate information available, whether it is a Web site, a CD-ROM, a pamphlet, a person, a database, a video, or a book.

Not very long ago, the research needs of students could be satisfied with a library catalog, several reference books, and perhaps a print or electronic periodical index. Currently, students have online access to other library catalogs, numerous periodical indexes, and a myriad of Web sites. As a school library media specialist, you must understand that students, when faced with a wide array of choices, will often choose what is easiest to use or what is familiar. Gaining skills in information literacy multiplies the opportunities for students' self-directed learning; they become engaged in using a wide variety of information sources, ask informed questions, and sharpen their critical thinking skills. As a school library media specialist, you can significantly contribute to information literacy in a way that no other member of the educational community can do. You can ensure the successful integration of information literacy skills within the curriculum and become a keystone in preparing students for success in the information age.

RESEARCH AND DEVELOPMENT

Although information literacy and how it applies to school library media specialists (and ultimately students, schools, and the community) has produced widespread research and literature, much more remains to be unveiled, learned, and discussed. According to Ellis and Lenk (2001), "As the information explosion and the burgeoning of new technologies have preoccupied the attention of educators, an increasing number of articles devoted to integrating technology into the curriculum have been published. Regrettably, the trend in these publications has been to overlook the obvious connection of libraries with classrooms with technology" (p. 12). Fortunately, however, this tendency within literature and educational practice to neglect the key role of school library media specialists is not universal. One excellent counterexample can be found in the 1998 publication of *Information Power: Building Partnerships for Learning:* "School library media specialists are now recognized as 'teacher' and 'instructional partner'" (AASL & AECT, 1998, p. 62). Riedling (2001a) conducted research in an attempt to define the roles of school library media specialists and discovered that most duties align with the information presented in *Information Power: Building Partnerships for Learning*. One primary component that clearly appears is that school library media specialists must be leaders—leaders in teaching information literacy skills to students, teachers, and the school community. Numerous other individuals involved with school library media centers have stated their opinions regarding where we are and where we should go concerning information literacy. Linda Langford (2001) says, "I believe that Industrial Age schooling must crumble and give rise to a more student-centered, goal-oriented, caring environment, which fosters active involvement and risk-taking, and ongoing personal mastery" (p. 18). As explained by Kysow, Shrive, Sihota, and Weichel (2003), the current-day school library media specialist should be extremely well equipped to provide leadership and collaborative planning in the implementation of a much-needed information literacy framework.

The literature reveals that we understand that information overload does exist. According to the Reuters Guide to Good Information Strategy (2000), more information has been produced during the last 30 years than during the previous 5,000 years. Wurman (1989) claims that the weekday edition of the *New York Times* contains more information than the average person in seventeenth-century England was likely to come across in a lifetime. Lyman (2000) explains that it is clear that we are all drowning in a sea of information. The challenge is to learn to swim in that sea, rather than sink under it. Better understanding and better tools are desperately needed if we are to take full advantage of the ever-increasing supply of information.

Jacobson (1997) remarks that if a theme runs through the research literature on contemporary practice in library and information studies (including information literacy), it is the centrality of concern for the library user. This is good news because students should be our main concern—our lifeline as a school library media specialist. This is particularly true within the arena of information literacy and the role school library media specialists must play regarding the teaching of this vital phenomenon. It is not always a clear-cut or simple task, but a critical one for students' success in today's world. Entwistle (1981) states that perhaps the biggest challenge for school library media specialists lies in planning and implementing a coherent program of instruction that not only meets the needs of students with vastly diverse computer skills, search experience, and interests, but also encourages deep rather than surface understanding of the processes involved. A primary goal of education is to make students independent, lifelong learners. To fully develop information literacy, students must be willing to come to school libraries. A study conducted by Mikalishen (2001) revealed that there is much that individuals (school library media specialists) should consider in making their facilities more user friendly. They should actively demonstrate that students are a priority. This means asking students what help they need when they come to the school library media center and providing it in a cheerful, supportive manner. It also means being perceptive as to what skills or knowledge students may lack in order to effectively access and work with the information they require. School library media specialists can use this student concern as a teachable moment to help a student work with information in a meaningful manner. In this way, students will also come to understand that school library media specialists actively support their learning (p. 22).

"In the year 2000, 60% of all jobs in the United States demanded information literacy skills, so it is our mission to make the public, administrators, parents and teachers understand how important a quality library media program is to students' future successes. It is [the school media specialists'] 'job' to help these groups understand that information literacy is the ability to find, select, analyze, and communicate information from a wide variety of print, nonprint, and electronic sources. It is our *duty* to show that the Internet is just *one* of a vast many tools that students are expected to be able to use, both in the workplace and for leisure activities. It is our position to let them know that the only people who are expert in all of these skill areas are school library media specialists" (Mohn, 2000, p. 33). Indeed, a large portion of teaching students to become information literate rests on the shoulders of school library media specialists. Pascale (1990) remarks that school library media specialists that make waves and spark contention—leaders—are regarded as assets, not liabilities. You, as a school library media specialist, must make waves and spark contention to create a nation of independent, lifelong learners. Thompson and Henley (2002) remark, "Information literate students do not necessarily know a lot of facts; they do know how to find answers and solve problems. An information literate student's knowledge base consists of information resources, search strategies, evaluation tips, organizing skills, and problem-solving processes that span all curriculum subjects and ultimately are more valuable than specific facts" (p. 2). Smith (1987) says that research has extended our understanding of the importance of collaboration between the library media specialist and teachers in integrating electronic resources into curricular units. Research also indicates the importance of knowledgeable school library media specialists—professionals who not only understand the techniques for online searching but also possess an understanding of the possibilities and idiosyncrasies of online resources (Thomas, 1991). As Hopkins (1999) stated in the article *Issues in the education of school library media specialists,* "collaboration, leadership and technology are seen as the underlying themes for guiding the school library media specialists in developing an effective, student-centered program. The three themes are intrinsically interrelated. To collaborate and lead effectively, library media specialists must possess the information technology skills necessary for providing aggressive information literacy education. The abundance of information and the complexity of new information structures require that students be information literate" (p. 88). Ultimately, the following is true: To plan collaboratively with teachers and to be recognized as instructional leaders, school library media specialists should have the competencies to guide and assist others in becoming information literate. The power to create communities of learners who are able to share information, ideas, and projects begins with enabling teachers and students to use technology as part of their daily educational experiences.

During the past half-century, there have been approximately 75 studies regarding the impact of school library media programs on academic achievement. Lance (2001a) explains, "Many early studies of this topic demonstrated the value of the mere presence of a professionally trained and credentialed [school] library media specialist. Such correlations, however, beg the question of what the school library media specialists are doing that makes a difference. In more recent studies, their contributions as creators of and collaborators in a learning community have been the focus" (p. 14). Lance continues to explain that all of the recent studies of the impact of school library media programs on academic achievement provide evidence to support several common findings: (1) Professionally trained and credentialed school library media specialists do make a difference that affects student performance on achievement tests. (2) For school library media specialists to make this difference, the support of principals and teachers is vital. (3) School library media specialists cannot perform their jobs effectively unless they have support staff that frees them from routine tasks and enables them to participate in a variety of one-to-one and group meetings outside the library media center. (4) School library media specialists have a twofold teaching role: they are teachers of students, facilitating the development of information-literacy skills necessary for success in all content areas, and they are in-service trainers of teachers, keeping abreast of the latest information resources and technology. (5) School library media specialists also must embrace technology to be effective. They must ensure that school networks extend the availability of information resources beyond the walls of the library media center, throughout the building, and in the best cases, into students' homes. Todd (1999) explains that the concept of evidence-based practice, that is, professional practice built on the explicit and judicious use of current best research findings in making decisions about the performance of the day-to-day role, and where the day-to-day professional work is directed towards demonstrating the tangible impacts and outcomes of sound decision making and implementation of organizational goals and objectives is vital in today's world. In 2003, Todd and Kuhlthau researched what is now known as the "Student Learning through Ohio School Libraries" study. These researchers collected quantitative and qualitative data from 13,123 students in grades 3 through 12 in 39 schools across Ohio. The students documented 10,316 statements. Here is an example: "I needed to write a paper, and I went to the library where I was ultimately able to write a paper successfully." This is a powerful statement regarding what school libraries can do.

From research and development, you can see that information literacy and the role that the school library media specialist plays regarding information literacy is gaining recognition and momentum. Research has now proven that effective school library media programs can increase student achievement—as well as information literacy—and result in students who are independent, socially responsible, lifelong learners.

The following resources will assist you in keeping abreast of current research and thinking regarding information literacy.

PRINT

Allen, C., & Anderson, M. A. (Eds.). (2001). Skills for life: Information literacy for grades K–6 *(2nd ed.). Worthington, OH: Linworth. This book is a collection of instructional guides developed by library media and technology specialists (appropriate for grades K–6).*

Allen, C., & Anderson, M. A. (Eds.). (2001). Skills for life: Information literacy for grades 7–12 *(2nd ed.). Worthington, OH: Linworth. This book provides guides developed by library media and technology specialists (appropriate for grades 7–12).*

Andronik, C. (1999). Information literacy skills, grades 7–12 *(3rd ed.). Worthington, OH: Linworth. This book reflects the technological changes of the past 10 years and combines concepts and theories on information seeking with specific lessons and applications.*

Barron, D. D. (2001). Thanks for the connections: Now are we information literate? School Library Media Activities Monthly, *18(3), 49–51. This article discusses Internet access in public schools, home access to computers, and the role of libraries in promoting information access and information literacy.*

Baule, S. (1998). "Information Power" prepares library media programs for a new age. Book Report, *17(3), 14–15. This article provides goals that help focus the library media program on the premise that the learning community must be focused on student needs.*

Donham, J., Bishop, K., Kuhlthau, C., & Oberg, D. (2001). Inquiry-based learning: Lessons from Library Power. *Worthington, OH: Linworth. Through theory, principles, research, and concrete examples, this book illustrates how the Library Power initiative can move your school toward an inquiry-based approach to teaching, learning, and curriculum renewal.*

Eisenberg, M., Lowe, C., & Spitzer, K. (2004). Information literacy: Essential skills for the information age *(2nd ed.). Englewood, CO: Libraries Unlimited. Tracing the history of information literacy, this book discusses its economic importance; examines past, present and current research in the field; and explains how information literacy relates to national standards.*

Farmer, L. S. J. (2002). Harnessing the power in information power. Teacher Librarian, *29(3), 20–25. This article discusses how the teacher-librarian identifies information literacy and library pro-gram needs.*

Grassian, E., & Kaplowitz, J. (2001). Information literacy instruction: Theory and practice. *New York: Neal-Schuman. This book discusses both theories and practices of library instruction; it includes an interactive CD-ROM.*

McKenzie, J. (2000). Beyond technology: Questioning, research, and the information literate school. *Worthington, OH: Linworth. This book makes information literacy the prime purpose for networking classrooms. It shows you how to transform your school into an information literate school community.*

Martin, A., & Rader, H. (Eds.). (2003). Information and IT literacy: Enabling learning in the 21st century. *New York: Neal-Schuman. This book converges IT and information skills literacy and provides surveys and analyzes current practice, emerging directions and ongoing issues.*

Serim, F. C. (2003). Information technology for learning: No school left behind. *Worthington, OH: Linworth. This book discusses the formation of information and technology teams to harness the power of IT to support good teaching with research-based practice.*

Thompson, H. M., & Henley, S. A. (2000). Fostering information literacy: Connecting National Standards, Goals 2000, and the SCANS Report. *Englewood, CO: Libraries Unlimited. This book shows the relationship between information literacy standards and national subject area curriculum standards.*

Whelan, D. L. (2003). *Why isn't information literacy catching on?* School Library Journal, 49(9), 50–54. *This article presents the results of a survey by* School Library Journal *about information literacy.*

NONPRINT

ACRL Institute for Information Literacy *[Online]. Available: http://www.ala.org/acrl/nili/nilihp.html. This helpful Web site offers the following, "If you have conducted or are planning to conduct a research study that explores a topic related to the library media field, please email me at drruth@twcny.rr.com and tell me*

*about it, briefly describing your methodology, where and with
whom the study will be conducted, what you hope to learn from
your study, and some preliminary results (if you have them)."*
What more could one ask for?

Age of the Information Literate *[Online]. Available: http://www.
clickz.com/design/site_design/article.php/837101. This article is
written by Gerry McGovern, who states, "Those who are running
for cover and sneering at the Internet are huddling in the past. The
Internet is big. There is blood on the tracks, sure. That's a necessary shedding of youthful skin. The Internet is maturing; it's going
to get bigger, badder, and better, and it will blow away those who
think they can live and work without it."*

Building Information Literacy *[Online]. Available: http://www.
edu.pe.ca/bil. This site explains the following: "Teaching and
learning in an information-rich, knowledge-based society; information literacy and resource-based learning; roles for school
libraries, information technology, and reading; roles for teacher-
librarians, classroom/subject teachers, students, administrators,
parents."*

*Grimble, B. J., & Williams, T. D. (2004, January). Students' percep-
tions of their information literacy skills in the media center.*
Library Media Connection *[Online]. Available: http://www.lin-
worth.com/lmc.html. This article discusses how students actually
perceive themselves as information users in a school library media
center.*

Information Power: Building Partnerships for Learning's Nine
Standards of Information Literacy *[Online]. Available:
http://www.ala.org/aasl/ip_nine.html. This Web site states the
nine standards of information literacy, as written in* Information
Power: Building Partnerships for Learning.

National Forum on Information Literacy *[Online]. Available:
http://www.infolit.org. "The National Forum on Information
Literacy was created in 1990 as a response to the recommendations of the American Library Association's Presidential Committee on Information Literacy. These education, library, and
business leaders stated that no other change in American society
has offered greater challenges than the emergence of the Information Age."*

Understanding Information Literacy *[Online]. Available: http:// www.ed.gov/pubs/UnderLit. This Web site covers the following topics: "Understanding Information Literacy; What Is Information Literacy?; Why Should We Be Concerned About Information Literacy?; Implications for Teaching; Implications for Learning; Implications for Schools; Implications for Libraries and Librarians; Implications for the Workplace; Implications for Society and Culture; Endnotes and References."*

WHAT'S HAPPENING

Now that the thrust of technological materials has been absorbed into the school environment, it is time to recognize the critical role of the school library media specialist as integrating, encouraging, and promoting these resources to the school's (student's) best advantage. Advances in information technology are advantageous in the school environment mainly because they forward the ultimate goal of producing information literate, independent, lifelong learners (Ellis & Lenk, 2001). How does a school library media specialist advertise information literacy? Unfortunately, there is no one, straightforward, and complete answer. Promoting and supporting information literacy in a school library media center requires knowledge, time, persistence, enthusiasm, and tenacity. As a school library media specialist, you must think creatively about your roles in student learning. School library media centers and school library media specialists often struggle with marketing, as evidenced by students' ignorance of the school library media center's basic services and resources, and by our enduring, stereotyped image as a school librarian. According to Rockwell-Kincanon (2001), "If we really want to push the concept of information literacy into the mainstream, and be identified as a major player in the movement, we need to pay attention to some 'media literacy' issues and take cues from current marketing tactics" (p. 16). To summarize Rockwell-Kincanon's remarks, good marketers are able to boil down their services to key concepts that attract their target audiences' attention and that remain memorable past the actual advertisement. The point of marketing is to grab attention and to give the students basic information so they realize that they want or need this product (information literacy skills). Actually, the school library media world is not without its good advertisement campaigns. The Celebrity READ series is quite enticing, as is the @ YOUR LIBRARY campaign released by the ALA's Campaign for American Libraries. Rockwell-Kincanon goes on to explain, "We can promote information literacy with humor, the surprise of familiar images combined with unexpected ones, and the use of strong visuals" (p. 17). To paraphrase Rockwell-Kincanon, marketing libraries and, specifically, information literacy, does not mean that we need to dumb down our point. The purpose of advertising is to catch the audience's attention. Our teaching colleagues, students, and the public still primarily see libraries as rule-based, unequivocal, orderly, and linear institutions. When we perform our jobs well, we make library work look incredibly easy. A challenge for us is to convince our students that school library media centers are flexible and spontaneous and, as such, are able to contribute to student learning. We (school library media specialists) can stretch the perceptions of what we do and more accurately reflect our modern selves by attempting daring and creative marketing campaigns (2001).

Before continuing with specific development and promotion activities, it is important to recall or reinforce what constitutes an information literate student. According to Doyle (1994), an information literate student is one who

> Recognizes that accurate and complete knowledge is the basis for
>   intelligent decision making
> Identifies the need for information
> Formulates questions based on information needs
> Identifies potential sources of information
> Develops successful search strategies
> Accesses sources of information including computer-based and
>   other technologies
> Evaluates information
> Organizes information for practical application
> Integrates new information into an existing body of knowledge
> Uses information in critical thinking and problem solving

"Ultimately, information literate people are those who have learned how to learn . . . because they can always find the information they need for any task or decision at hand" (ALA, 1998, p. 8).

Now, let's get practical—and look at the who, what, when, where, why, and how again—this time regarding producing and developing information literate individuals.

Who? This answer is relatively simple—learners—whoever they are!

What? This requires teaching information literacy skills to students (and possibly to teachers, other school personnel, and the community). Precise information literacy skills to teach and develop are included in the remaining chapters.

When? Teaching information literacy skills is an ongoing process. There is no beginning or end—it just is and will be. You might teach students and teachers on an individual basis; you may perhaps teach in small or large groups, or even provide in-service activities. Actually, teach it at every possible moment! Information literacy skills are independent, lifelong skills that can be taught within any curriculum area and in any environment. This is an important aspect of teaching information literacy skills.

Where? The teaching of information literacy skills can take place anywhere—because information is everywhere! Information literacy touches every avenue of living, so it can be taught anywhere—in the media center, in a classroom, outside, on field trips, and so forth. Instruction about information literacy skills should be taught in collaboration—with teachers (primarily)—and other school personnel, as well as in the total school environment. However, most likely, the teaching of these skills will take place in the school library media center and/or classroom.

Why? The *why* of teaching information literacy has been previously defined. However, remember that you, a school library media specialist, are the key component in teaching these skills—you have the knowledge, expertise, resources, and, one hopes, the enthusiasm and energy!

How? This question will be answered (in part) later. Remember, however, that these are *merely examples* of how you can teach information literacy skills—the rest is up to your creativity and endless imagination! Breivik and Senn (1994) explain, "to achieve information literacy, students must be given repeated opportunities to work with the same information resources that will bombard them throughout their lives. To help their students become information literate, teachers—supported by school library media specialists—must move away from single-text teaching and focus on exposing students to real-world information resources and technologies" (p. 11). The following are examples of *lesson ideas* that incorporate information literacy skills within content skills instruction in other curriculum areas:

Information Literacy Goals

> *Students will access Web-based reference materials efficiently and effectively.*
> *Students will evaluate Web-based information resources and choose materials appropriately.*
> *Students will use Web-based information creatively in producing their project.*

Information Literacy Objectives

> *Students will create questions based on their specific information needs.*
> *Students will select Web-based materials that best answer their questions.*
> *Students will synthesize information from a variety of Web-based resources.*
> *Students will create a finished project using the information gathered.*

Language Arts/English Course Objectives

> *Students will demonstrate the ability to use the online databases: SIRS Renaissance (via SIRS); Biography Index (via FirstSearch); and Academic Search Premier (via EBSCO).*
> *Students will create summarizations and paraphrases (with appropriate citations) regarding the Web-based information they have located.*

> *Students will condense the information and synthesize that information into a logical report.*
>
> Science Course Objectives
>
> *Students will demonstrate the ability to use the following online databases: Geobase (via FirstSearch); AGRICOLA (via First Search); and EBSCO Animals (via EBSCO).*
> *Students will select an endangered species. Using the databases, they will accumulate appropriate information (taking notes, summarizing, and so forth) about this animal (where it lives, eating habits, mating habits, etc.).*
> *Students will synthesize this information and create a paper explaining a procedure for making this animal no longer an endangered species.*

For these lessons, the school library media specialist works closely with the language arts and science teachers. They determine their specific duties, a timeline, and so forth. These are just two examples of developing and promoting information literacy skills. By providing guidance and appropriate resources, the school library media specialist instills independent learning. In addition, the teacher learns about the use of databases and the school library media specialist saves the teacher's time, as well as providing information literacy skills for students. Actually, it is not so much a matter of purposely turning away from an old teaching approach as it is of incorporating a resource-based approach to learning over time (step-by-step). In other words, we must first show—students, teachers, and the school community—the urgent need for information literacy skills and then, once we have caught their attention—shown them that this is necessary to survive in today's society—we assist them to create students who are independent, lifelong learners. *That is our job (one of them!) as a school library media specialist in the twenty-first century.*

2

In the School

INTRODUCTION

How can school library media specialists make information literacy skills important to teachers and students, while actually teaching them something meaningful about the Internet? There is no doubt that you—*alone*—as the school library media specialist—cannot instill *all* of the information literacy skills in each student and teacher in your school. You are not superhuman, nor are you expected to be. What you *can* do, however, is to teach the *importance* of these skills and direct students and teachers to the path of lifelong, independent learning. This chapter is all about collaborating to make a difference, selling information literacy, *making information literacy a schoolwide reform effort*. We continue to seek effective ways for students to learn. As Wolcott (1994) stated, "Recent literature concerning the role of school library media programs in the 'information age' reverberates with several themes: information literacy, critical thinking, and resource-based learning. These themes emphasize the changing role of the school library media specialist—one that is characterized as an instructional partnership between teachers and the school library media specialist" (p. 1). As stated in *Information Power: Building Partnerships for Learning* (AASL & AECT, 1998),

The school library media specialist in an instructional consult action role is responsible for the following:

Participating in school, district, departmental, and grade level curriculum design and assessment projects

Helping teachers develop instructional activities

Providing expertise in the selection, evaluation, and use of materials and emerging technologies for the delivery of information and instruction

Translating curriculum needs into school library media program goals and objectives. (p. 4)

It is our responsibility—our duty—as *leaders* in teaching information literacy skills to create independent, information literate, lifelong learners *in collaboration with teachers and the school community.* This chapter will outline and describe the process of school library media specialist/teacher collaboration, provide examples of such collaborative efforts, explain one popular information problem solving model (Eisenberg's & Berkowitz's Big6 model), and discuss current thinking and research regarding collaboration and information literacy across the school.

COLLABORATION

Collaboration sounds easy—just *explain* to the teacher that students need to learn information literacy skills (maybe even provide them with a handout) and collaborate, right? Wrong—if it were *only that simple!* Let's back up a step or two. Why *can't* you teach information literacy skills *all alone?* How many times a week do you see each student in the school library media center? How many *minutes* do you have to work with each student individually per week—15 minutes, 10 minutes, sometimes none? I believe you are beginning to get the picture. So, now you agree that teaching information literacy skills—access, use, evaluation, and so forth—*should* be and *needs* to be accomplished *with* your teachers (and other school community members). Why doesn't everyone else get the picture? According to the ALA (1998),

[Collaborative] benefits include a wide variety of 'plusses' or positives relating to libraries and partnerships and collaborations. Those reviewing the list, however, should note the following statements:

Not everyone views or values 'benefits' in the same way. What is
a benefit to one type of school library media center or in one
part of the country may not be a benefit elsewhere.

Just as political agendas, administrations, services and members of the public change, so do benefits. That is, what works
well and what benefits are realized under one leader may not
work or be realized under another.

Projects have 'lives,' that is a project may live and be successful
and grow and then the project, activity, service or partnership may die a natural death." (p. 1)

That's not particularly good news, is it? All right, first let's look at
some benefits of collaboration—to you, the teachers, the students, and
the school community. The following are examples:

A greater knowledge base of people who "know" what the school
library media center is and what it can do.

Recognition of the wide variety of roles and responsibilities that
school library media specialists play in the life of the school as a
whole.

Provision of consistent and effective instruction in the twenty-
first century regarding lifelong, independent learning.

A smarter, more prepared twenty-first-century citizenry.

A more knowledgeable student/teacher/other, which sees opportunities in information environments and maximizes resources.

The fact that "everyone knows what everyone else is doing."

The creation of a network of people to make things happen.

The development of independent, lifelong learners to move forth
in society.

Is collaboration worth all of the effort—YOU BET!! As stated
repeatedly, our society and culture demands people who are independent, socially responsible, lifelong learners. It requires that people
understand information and are able to use it successfully. Where else
would one learn these skills but in school? And who is better equipped
than *you and the teachers and school community* to provide this for students? School library media specialist can best teach information literacy skills in the context of the curriculum. It is an easier task if the

school library media specialist's assists the teacher and explains the benefits—overall saving of time, thinking of the vested interests of students (information literate, independent, socially responsible, independent learners), and so forth. As Tschamler (2002) explained, "I worked collaboratively with a teacher to teach information skills to a class of students. Without collaboration, there would be no framework for teaching the information skills that are a part of the school's curriculum. Because no one simply uses information skills without having a purpose or reason, collaboration provides an opportunity to create a purpose in conjunction with a lesson, in order to teach students the value of information and research skills. Once students are motivated to learn these skills, they are well on their way to becoming independent thinkers and lifelong learners" (p. 14). *I could not have said it better!* Mikalishen (2001), a school librarian from Canada, discusses a research study carried out by a "teacher-librarian" (school library media specialist). The overall project was designed to determine what services and resources [school library media specialists] are currently offering that are effective in supporting the acquisition of information literacy skills. Two important comments resulted from this project regarding information literacy and the role of the school library media specialist:

> The teachers who described very positive experiences in teaming with [school library media specialists] to work with their classes on various aspects of information literacy almost always identified time to plan and communicate expectations as being the single most important contributing factor to success.
>
> [School library media specialists] should actively demonstrate that students are a priority. This means asking students what help they need when they come to the library and providing it in a cheerful, supportive manner. It also means being perceptive as to what skills or knowledge students may lack in order to effectively access and work with the information they require... [School library media specialists] can use this student concern as a teachable moment to help a student work with information in meaningful ways. In this way students will also come to understand that [school library media specialists] actively support their learning..." (p. 22)

A study was conducted at Cornell University regarding the library/information technology director at Berkeley Carol School in New York. Seventy-six K–12 schools were surveyed via the Web to learn more about the status of school library media programs and the integration of information technology and information literacy in schools. This study discovered that school library media specialists were performing the bulk of information technology and literacy integration. More importantly, the survey discovered that although most schools have fully embraced the use of information technology, only 38 percent of the schools reported having a *schoolwide effort* for incorporating information literacy into the curriculum. This study concluded with a *summary of key recommendations:*

Mandate a cohesive, schoolwide plan for an information literacy curriculum.

Provide more time for and encourage collaboration among teachers, school library media specialists, and technology coordinators in the development of research-based learning projects.

Ensure that school library media specialists are part of the academic committee(s) that reviews all major curricula.

Move away from the more traditional research assignments, such as fact gathering and reporting, to assignments requiring understanding and interpretation of ideas and information.

Similarly, school library media specialists were polled regarding ways to initiate collaboration with teachers and administrators (Department of Defense Education Activities [DoDEA] Conference, March, 2004). They are as follows:

Entice teachers with pre-designed lesson plans

Invite teachers to the school library to share food and information about upcoming resources

Offer to help with planning and implementing thematic units

Offer to work with a teacher who has challenging students

Pull related content materials and offer to co-teach a unit

Spotlight collaboration accomplished at a faculty meeting

Use the personal touch

Meet with departments and grade level teams/Visit teachers on their turf

Advertise successes/Create excitement

Use curriculum mapping—be ready with materials at the right moment

Share lessons you have done before (and articles, Web sites, ideas, etc.)

Get kids involved

Gain support from your administration

Locate willing teachers

Show and tell of an effective co-teaching unit/collaborative activities/ Show best practices (maybe even a CD!)

Develop a curriculum calendar

Be knowledgeable of the curriculum and query teacher needs

Visit classes/ Kibitz . . . talk . . . chat . . . plan . . .

Advertise your assets/Share student work in display cases in the school library

Keep copies of textbooks (teachers' editions) in the library media center

Provide teacher information via email

Make teachers look good

Check material request forms and make suggestions

Offer after-school training

Provide a newsletter with technology tips

Have a party/Wine and dine!

Take time/Allot time to advertise on teacher workdays

Use public relations—door prizes, recognition/ Provide rewards

ALWAYS say "thank you!"

Assist with effective assessments

Be proactive and seize the moments

Tie into special projects

Use the technology committee to promote collaboration

Request in-service/professional development days—with release time for collaboration

Find a champion for the cause/Target receptive teachers

Provide leadership and fellowship/Lead by example

Provide a list of people resources available in the community

Give MLA/APA citation presentations and lessons

Make a promotional video

Gather data (research) that supports collaboration

Be persistent, patient, and pleasant

Start small, make it easy, and do not scare them!

Create a collaboration folder and place it on email

Check around and see what others are doing/ Read literature about collaboration to gain ideas

Provide webliographies

Get quarterly overview plans from teachers

Be positive and be seen as a team maker

Keep lines of communication open

Be personable and give teachers ownership

Get recommendations for materials (teacher requests)

Take your show on the road

Grab opportunities and build on impulse

Tie in with Big6/Super3 lessons

Request to perform book talks in classrooms

Provide techtime once a month to showcase resources

Be involved with the school/Be available and visible

Anticipate needs

Understand and accommodate different personalities and teaching/ learning styles

Post a weekly Web site update about collaboration

Eat lunch with teachers and administrations—to learn

Make collaboration FUN!

Be willing to share responsibilities

Work cooperatively by relieving their workload

Show teachers you can save them time

Chocolate encouragement!

The following is an example of "A Collaborative Planning Scenario."

(WLMA [Washington Library Media Association] Ad Hoc Committee on Essential Learnings, 2004)

A COLLABORATIVE PLANNING SCENARIO

Preconference

Before beginning a collaborative planning project with a staff member, do some pre-conferencing with yourself. Think about the following:

What is the common ground the teacher and I share?

Listening to what the teacher needs

Being adaptable to teacher's needs

Planning is usually a solitary activity for most teachers—how can I help without dominating the process?

Finding out what the teacher means when he/she says "research." (Ask probing questions.)

Making the first move—ask the teacher to plan with you.

Conference

THE RAIN FOREST PROJECT

Note: Resources will vary according to grade level and collection

What is the topic and what kinds of projects can be done? How can higher order thinking skills be incorporated? Get into as many specifics as possible; provide guidance in the structure of the assignment. If you both know what the end products should look like, you'll avoid opportunities for plagiarism.

Rain Forest study project topics will be generated by class discussion, student desire, and teacher suggestion.

What do you want the students to know and do? What specific Essential Learnings does this project address? What Information Literacy Skills are addressed?

What resources does the library have?

Check library collection in Reference, 500's, 600's, 900's, Vertical files, SIRS, Reader's Guide to Periodical Literature, National Geographic Index, and Biography (if filed as a separate section of the collection). CD's, laser discs, the Internet, and other electronic resources for rain forest, biomes, environment, jungles, forests and forestry, and the names of specific plants and animals of the rain forest... .

What resources can we get from the ESD, the local public library, the local college or university?

Look through the Instructional materials catalog under the topics rain forest, jungles, environment, biomes, jungles, forest and forestry, and the names of specific plants and animals of the rain forest... Check some areas in the local public library, the local college or university public access catalogs.

What skills do the students need to complete the assignment? What are the various levels of ability and learning styles which must be accommodated? Who will assess the skills of the individual students? Who will assess the skills of the individual students? Who will be responsible for teaching basic skills? How will the unit/assignment be introduced? Where will we incorporate re-teaching time and provide the break for mid-course corrections? Who will teach what, and where will the teaching take place? In the classroom? In the library? In the computer lab? Elsewhere?

How long do students have to do the assignment? What is the time line? How many days do the students need in the library?

Bring a library calendar and schedule the time. Also schedule a time at the end of the unit for the teacher and the librarian to evaluate how their plan went.

How will we monitor the project?
How will students evaluate the experience and their finished product? How will we assess the unit?

Responsibilities

Students

Determined by the teacher and librarian to comply with the school's policy.

Demonstrates ability to use a variety of resources, print and non-print.

Produces a project (text, multimedia, video) dealing with some aspect of the Rain Forest to be determined by the teacher and the student.

Demonstrates ability to cite all sources correctly.

Teacher

Sets the parameters of the assignment.

Introduces the Rain Forest unit and sets the expectations for the projects.

Teaches the writing process necessary to support student project.

Sets and maintains the time line.

Monitors student use of the facility when whole class is in the library.

Checks for understanding and mastery through the use of section evaluations, student interview and observation.

Reinforces citation lesson.

Grades the final product for content and mastery of the target skills.

Ties in the content area Essential Learning.

Library Media Specialist

Presents a short library orientation to review area(s) specific to student's inquiry.

Reinforces Internet use policy with students, encourages responsible Internet use including basics of netiquette; provides assistance with Internet access.

Teaches search skills for text and various electronic and on-line sources.

Teaches citation of sources/in-class lecture and hands-on in classroom and library.

Tracks or manages resources for in-class and in-library sharing.

Monitors student use of facility whole class and drop-in situations.

Checks for understanding and mastery through the use of section evaluations, student interviews, and observation.

Reinforces or re-teaches citation form, writing formats, search techniques.

Introduces new sources or skills as students show a need.

Evaluates the final product for mastery of the citation form.

Displays the completed projects in the library.

Evaluation

Periodic conferences between teacher and librarian to monitor student progress and go over "what is going well" and "what we need to do differently."

Conferences with students to check for understanding and mastery.

Section evaluation sheets.

Evaluating the projects, joint conferencing.

Joint conference to evaluate the success of the whole project... what went well, what we would do again, what we need to change, etc.

Collaboration allows the school library media specialists to play a more active role in the curriculum and education of our students. Collaborating with teachers and administrators is the only way to ensure that information literacy skills will be learned within a meaningful context. *Collaboration is vital!*

PROBLEM-SOLVING STRATEGIES

What are information problem solving strategies and models? To describe it simply, they are steps or strategies to assist in conducting research. Why are they important? These models guide students logically through information and through research. Numerous models have been developed over the years. One model will be the primary focus of this chapter; however, let's look quickly at a few others to see what these models are and what they can do. Yucht (1997) developed an information skills strategy for student researchers called FLIP, which stands for

F	ocus on your topic
L	ocate the appropriate resources
I	nvestigate and Implement the Information you find
P	roduce the results of your findings

Cornell University developed *The Seven Steps of the Research Process,* which include:

Identify and develop your topic
Find background information
Use catalogs to find books
Use indexes to find periodical articles
Find Internet/audio and video resources
Evaluate what you find
Cite what you find using a standard format (2001)

Although this model is somewhat more detailed and complicated, it provides a useful strategy for conducting research. Finally, North High School Library developed yet another information problem solving model:

Define the topic
Collect information
Evaluate sources
Extract/synthesize information
Cite information
Present information
Reflect on your research

Again, this model differs slightly from others, but still provides a user-friendly outline for conducting research. Although each model explains the research process with different terms and emphasizes different phases of the process, they all seem to agree on the overall scope and general breakdown of the process. I hope that you are beginning to understand what this is all about! A well-known information problem-solving model used in K–12 schools is Eisenberg and Berkowitz's Big6™ Skills Research Model.

As stated by Eisenberg and Brown (1992),

> Instruction in library and information skills is widely accepted as one of the major functions of the [school] library media program. Support for this teaching role is found in the mission statement of *Information Power*...Four major themes about library and information skills instruction are assumed within these two statements. These themes represent widespread current beliefs about the value of library and information skills, the nature and scope of skills instruction, and effective approaches to teaching library and information skills:
>
> > Instruction in library and information skills is a valuable and vital part of the school's educational program.
> > Important library and information skills encompass more than just location of and access to sources. The skills curriculum should emphasize general information problem solving and research processes.
> > Library and information skills should not be taught in isolation. The skills program must be fully integrated with the school's curriculum.
> > The use of innovative instructional methods and technologies can enhance the teaching of library and information skills. (pp. 1–2)

The Big6 model makes it easier to see the connection between the research process and using Internet information sources effectively. The approach focuses on the process of solving information problems. It is a systematic approach to organizing information from a variety of sources. The Big6 model is regarded as an effective means for teachers to implement teaching and learning of information and technology skills into their curriculum to prepare students for the twenty-first century. The basic outline of the Big6 skills approach model is as follows:

Task Definition

> *Define the problem*
> *Define the information requirements of the problem*

Information Seeking Strategies

> *Determine the range of possible resources*
> *Evaluate the different possible resources to determine priorities*

Location and Access

> *Locate sources*
> *Find information within resources*

Use of information

> *Engage*
> *Extract information from a source*

Synthesis

> *Organize information from multiple sources*
> *Present information*

Evaluation

> *Judge the product*
> *Judge the information problem solving process*

Students today need to learn *what to do with* information, not just how to locate it. However, more research is needed to explore just how using these (and other similar skills) affect students immediately and in the future. Kuhlthau (1989) points out, "School library media specialists have difficulty measuring the impact of school library media center use on learning. Further research is required about the influence of information search processes on student products" (p. 23). To move from content-driven to an information-process-driven basis of instruction, it is important to learn more about the characteristics of high-quality instruction, such as the following:

Higher-order thinking skills
Repetition of good practices
Moving from teacher-dependent to independent student learning
  behaviors
Levels of learning: literal, interpretive, and applied

The Big6 model is both diagnostic and prescriptive. As school library media specialists, you should look at the process, as well as at student performance. Moving from tests to higher-order thinking requires a different framework for instruction. Hopsicker (1997), a social studies teacher in New York, states, "What I like about the Big6 is that you assume nothing and that it's really common sense. You just apply the common sense you use in everyday life to school things" (p. 17). School library media specialists know that Big6 skills and the national information literacy standards provide a powerful repertoire of research tools to integrate technology into every area of the curriculum. It is our challenge to share that understanding with our colleagues. Teachers who use the Big6 skills may acquire an appreciation of the national information literacy standards by seeing them in a familiar framework. Teachers who have not yet used the World Wide Web resources to support student research may be more enthusiastic if they can see the experience as a way to learn information problem-solving skills. Collaboration, once again, is essential. School library media specialists and teachers *must* work together to incorporate information problem solving in the school curricula. This collaboration results in meaningful and successful learning experiences. Furthermore, by using the Big6 model, students become experts in a process approach to problem solving. The Big6 model provides a plan of action as students seek to solve personal and school-related information problems. Collaboration is necessary for resource-based teaching and integrating information literacy skills. Using the Big6 model for cooperative planning with teachers reinforces the effectiveness of information problem-solving as part of the planning process.

Big6 Cooperative Planning Guide

Teacher/Grade Level _____

Content Area/Unit of Study _____

Estimated Time Frame _____

Indiana Academic Standards

- _____

- _____

- _____

- _____

Technology Used:

- ☐ Digital Camera
- ☐ Scanner
- ☐ Video Camera
- ☐ PowerPoint
- ☐ Internet
- ☐ Microsoft Publisher
- ☐ Kidspiratioon
- ☐ Encarta
- ☐ Microsoft Word
- ☐ Other _____

Information Literacy Standards

The student who is information literate:
- ☐ Accesses information efficiently and effectively
- ☐ Evaluates information critically and competently
- ☐ Uses information accurately and creatively

The student who is an independent learner is:
- ☐ Information literate and pursues information related to personal interests
- ☐ Information literate and appreciates literature and other creative expressions of information
- ☐ Information literate and strives for excellence in information seeking and knowledge generation

The student who contributes positively to the learning community and to society is:
- ☐ Information literate and recognized the importance of information to a democratic society
- ☐ Information literate and practices ethical behavior in regard to information and information technology
- ☐ Information literate and participates effectively in groups to pursue and generate information

STEP ONE: What do we want the students to do? Define the assignment. Determine what kind of product we want. How will we work out the necessary time?

STEP TWO: What resources will the students use? Which ones will be the best?

  Media Specialist Responsibility: Make a Project Pathfinder.

  Teacher's Responsibility:

STEP THREE: Where will students find these resources? How can we help them identify the right information they need? (What's relevant and what isn't)
>   Media Specialist's Responsibility:

>   Teacher's Responsibility:

STEP FOUR: How can we help them read, take notes and use the information?
>   Media Specialist's Responsibility:

>   Teacher's Responsibility

STEP FIVE: How can we help them organize the information into a product?
>   Media Specialist's Responsibility:

>   Teacher's Responsibility:

STEP SIX: How will we evaluate the student work? Will we use a rubric? Will students also evaluate themselves?
>   Media Specialist's Responsibility:

>   Teacher's Responsibility:

RESEARCH AND DEVELOPMENT

Recent literature shows that we are moving in the right direction regarding teaching information literacy skills—and teaching them *in collaboration* and *across the school curriculum.* Johnson (1999) constructed a combined library and technology curriculum that is a true information literacy curriculum. This would accomplish the following:

> The curriculum would be based on projects that resulted in products using a variety of media and formats.
>
> The curriculum would teach useful technology skills primarily using productivity software.
>
> Information literacy skills, rather than library skills, would help students learn how to use information, as well as how to find it.
>
> Student research would ask for original higher level thinking, helping teachers and librarians combat both plagiarism and boredom.
>
> The projects would be integrated into the classroom's content areas and be team taught by the school library media specialist and the classroom teacher.
>
> The projects would be authentically assessed, and the tools used to design those assessments would serve as models for other areas of the curriculum.
>
> Students would learn core technology skills that would allow them to be productive....

To achieve these goals, a nine-step process was put in place:

> Identify current skills...
>
> Identify and learn an information processing model...
>
> Group skills within the process...
>
> Identify areas in the curriculum for integration...
>
> Brainstorm projects...
>
> Identify needed resources...
>
> Develop assessment tools...
>
> Develop a record-keeping and reporting system...
>
> Review and revise....

Most important, Johnson found

> It was critical to involve others, especially teachers, as we developed the curriculum:
>
>> The impetus for the curricular change came from a group representing a wide segment of both the school and the community...
>>
>> Collaboration and dialogue between [school library] media specialists and teachers were critical to integrating information literacy into the curriculum...

This project is important for us to recognize and comprehend. This is merely how one district developed a collaborative curriculum that taught information literacy skills. It may not be easy, but it is achievable; this is just *one* possible method!

A book written in 2001 by Jenny Ryan and Steph Capra, entitled *Information Literacy Toolkit,* again shows the great strides we have made regarding collaboration and information literacy. This book creates a new way of thinking about research skills for both librarians and teachers and includes teaching tools applicable across grade and curriculum units. Another book, entitled *The Information Literate School Community*, includes a collection of research, professional, and case study papers that explore a wide range of issues and open a window of understanding to what has been dubbed a fuzzy concept—information literacy (Henri & Bonanno, 1999). This concept is being progressively recognized as a critical issue in education, workplace, and community. Buzzeo (2002a & 2002b) wrote two books concerning collaboration (for differing grade levels), *Collaborating to Meet Standards: Teacher/Librarian Partnerships for K–6* [and *for 7–12*]. Her supplementary, "how-to" books explain, "Collaboration is much more than just the latest buzzword. It is a worthwhile concept that can greatly benefit library media specialists, teachers, students, and administrators alike. And *if it is* done correctly, collaborative planning and teaching can help with meeting education standards" (2002a, p. 6).

A slightly different slant on information literacy and collaboration is that of school library media specialists teaching teachers how to create research projects (questioning) that dissuade plagiarism. As stated by Rankin (1996), "Despite our best efforts with students, we will always swim upstream if we do not also help teachers establish conditions that support quality work. There are many ways to do this; the approach you take will often depend on the teacher you are working with and the degree to which you are working together" (p. 148). According to Riedling (2001b), "Teachers and library media specialists must learn to develop questions that discourage 'find it and print it' processes. Higher-level questions ask students to mentally manipulate pieces of information previously learned to create an answer or to support and answer with logical evidence. They require comparing and contrasting, predicting, evaluating, hypothesizing, reconstructing, inferring, judging, defending, and valuing by students.... Powerful questioning leads to information power, the ability to fashion solutions, decisions, and plans that are original, cogent, and effective. Powerful questions are the foundation for information literacy. Higher-level questions encourage students to think more deeply and critically, to problem solve, and to seek information on their own" (p. 29).

The teaching of information literacy skills requires a *team.* For years, this was thought to be the sole responsibility of the school library media specialist. We can hope that it is now more apparent that teaching students to become independent, lifelong learners requires the efforts of the entire school community. These skills must touch and relate to all curriculum areas. As a school library media specialist, you are the *leader* in this endeavor, but remember that it cannot be accomplished—or accomplished well—in *isolation.* The following are additional readings and Web sites related to information literacy, collaboration, and teamwork:

PRINT

Barron, D. D. (2000). Change, collaboration, and cultures: Challenges for school library media specialist leaders (or, What's love got to do with it?). School Library Media Activities Monthly, 16(6), 47–50. This article focuses on numerous components of school library media and includes an "anti-formula formula" for dealing with change.

Berkowitz, R., & Serim, F. (2002). *Moving every child ahead: The Big6 success strategy.* Multimedia Schools, 9*(3), 16–21. This arti- cle discusses how the Big6 model assists new teachers in higher- order teaching and learning.*

Birks, J., & Hunt, F. (2003). Hands-on information literacy activi- ties. *New York: Neal-Schuman. This book is a comprehensive col- lection of interactive learning activities designed to develop information literacy skills.*

Buzzeo, T. (2002). Collaborating to meet standards: Teacher/ librarian partnerships for K–6. *Worthington, OH: Linworth. This book talks about collaboration between teachers, administra- tors, others and library media specialists to effectively communi- cate and meet standards (aimed for K–6 environment).*

Callison, D. (1999). *Key words in instruction: Collaboration.* School Library Media Activities Monthly, 15*(5), 38–40. This article dis- cusses the importance of collaboration for school library media programs and provides strategies to make collaboration successful.*

Callison, D. (2002). *Information inquiry.* School Library Media Activities Monthly, 8*(10), 35. This article deals with a learning method called information inquiry; it discusses components, related problems, questions, and so forth.*

Capra, S., & Ryan, J. (Eds.). (2002). Problems are the solution: Keys to lifelong learning. *Worthington, OH: Linworth. This book fosters critical thinking and problem-solving skills in students by using problem-based learning.*

Carr, J., & Rockman, I. F. (2003). *Information-literacy collabora- tion: A shared responsibility.* American Libraries, 34*(8), 52–55. This article discusses the collaboration between academic and K–12 libraries in the United States.*

Donham, J., Bishop, K., Kuhlthau, C., & Oberg, D. (2001). Inquiry- based learning: Lessons from Library Power. *Worthington, OH: Linworth. This book is based on real schools and the struggles of school library media specialists. It includes theory, principles, research, and concrete examples.*

Eisenberg, M. B., & Berkowitz, R. E. (1990). Information problem- solving: The Big6 skills approach to library and information skills. *Worthington, OH: Linworth. This book presents the Big6 in multiple perspectives and shows detailed applications of the Big6 model.*

Ellis, K. V. (2001). *Libraries and information literacy survey analysis.* Independent School, 60(4), 14–16. *This article discusses a Web survey regarding the status of library media programs and the integration of information technology and information literacy in independent schools.*

Farmer, L. S. J. (1999). *Making information literacy a school wide reform effort.* Book Report, 18(3), 6–8. *This article examines the Redwood High School's Bay Area School Reform collaborative, an educational reform project.*

Farmer, L. S. J. (1999). Partnerships for lifelong learning *(2nd ed.).* Worthington, OH: Linworth. *This book discusses being proactive and making educational partnerships happen.*

Fullner, S. (2002). Big6 & trade: Rap contest. Library Talk, 15(2), 28. *This article presents information on a rap contest for eighth graders at Noosak Valley Middle School in Washington and the related research strategies of the Big6 model.*

Hackman, M. H. (1999). Library information skills and the high school English program *(2nd ed.). Englewood, CO: Libraries Unlimited. This book provides practical ideas for integrating library information skills into the high school English curriculum.*

Harris, F. J. (2003). *Information literacy in school libraries: It takes a community.* Reference and User Services Quarterly, 42(3), 215–223. *The author of this article discusses how adult learners and adolescent learners perceive information literacy.*

Heller, N. (2001). Information literacy and technology research projects: Grades 6–9. *Englewood, CO: Libraries Unlimited. Through this book, students are educated about the new roles information technology can play in their quest for knowledge.*

Joseph, L. C. (2002). *Building prior knowledge.* Multimedia Schools, 9(3), 30–32. *This article focuses on the effectiveness of the Big6 framework in introducing information critical to learning.*

Kachel, D. E. (2003). *Partners for success: A school library advocacy training program for principals.* Knowledge Quest, 52(2), 17–19. *This article discusses the importance of administrative support for school library media specialists.*

Kasowitz, A. S. (2000). Using the Big6 to teach and learn the Internet. *Worthington, OH: Linworth. This book provides instruction and guidance to students solving information problems with various tools, including the Internet.*

Kresberg, S. (2001). *Faculty-library media specialist cooperation or collaboration.* School Library Media Activities Monthly, 18*(1),* 22–25. *This article discusses the terms* cooperation *and* collaboration *and how they can work together for faculty-library media specialists.*

Kuhlthau, C. C. (2002). Teaching the library research process: A step-by-step program for secondary school students *(2nd ed.). New York: Scarecrow Press. This book provides a complete instructional program for introducing secondary school students to the process of library research.*

Lane, N., Chisolm, M., & Mateer, C. (2000). Techniques for student research: A comprehensive guide to using the library. *New York: Neal-Schuman. This book offers in-depth strategies for confident, efficient, and effective information searching.*

Langhorn, M. J. (Ed.). (1998). Developing an information literacy program K–12: A how-to-do-it manual and CD-ROM package. *New York: Neal-Schuman. This manual provides a complete information literacy model with an accompanying interactive CD-ROM.*

Logan, D. K. (1999). Information skills toolkit: Collaborative integrated instruction for middle grades. *Worthington, OH: Linworth. This book uses a tested working toolkit to show how to integrate information skills instruction with content area curriculum.*

McKenzie, J. (2001). Planning good change with technology and literacy. *Worthington, OH: Linworth. This book is about making change that makes instruction better and that endures by combining technologies with an emphasis on literacy.*

Milam, P. (2002). InfoQuest: A new twist on information literacy. *Worthington, OH: Linworth. This book is designed to motivate students to do more research; it ensures that information literacy skills are continuously practiced.*

Minkel, W. (2002). Selling information literacy. School Library Journal, 48*(2), 37. This article discusses how to make information* literacy skills important to teachers and students while teaching students something meaningful about the Internet.

Riedling, A. M. (2001). *The question is the solution.* Book Report, 20(1), 28–29. *This article discusses how to use higher-order questioning to discourage plagiarism and to develop problem-solving skills.*

Russell, S. (2002). *Teachers and librarians: Collaborative relationships.* Teacher Librarian, 29(5), 35–38. *This article discusses establishing successful collaborative relationships between classroom teachers and library media specialists.*

Small, R. (2002). *Collaboration...* Teacher Librarian, 29(5), 8–11. *This article discusses the idea that collaboration has become the norm in most organizations; we work together face-to-face and virtually on common projects to satisfy clients or customers and to benefit the organization.*

Stripling, B. K., & Hassell, S. H. (Eds.). (2003). Curriculum connections through the library. *Englewood, CO: Libraries Unlimited. This book explores educational principles and research and connects national curriculum trends to current library practices.*

Thomas, N. P. (2004). Information literacy and information skills instruction *(2nd ed.). Englewood, CO: Libraries Unlimited. This book provides a review of the literature about information skills instruction.*

Troutner, J. (2001). *Web wonders.* Teacher Librarian, 28(5), 33. *This article provides information on several Web sites for information literacy ideas and teaching about search strategies.*

Wolinsky, A. (2002). Internet power research using the Big6 approach. *Worthington, OH: Linworth. This book provides school library media specialists, teachers, and students with an easy-to-follow Big6 method to solve research problems in the Internet age.*

Zweizig, D. L., Hopkins, D. M., Webb, N. L., & Wehlage, G. (1999). Lessons from library power. *Englewood, CO: Libraries Unlimited. This book discusses revitalizing school library media programs using a variety of approaches.*

NONPRINT

Big6 Matrix *[Online]. Available: http://www.surfline.ne.jp/janetm/
   big6info.htm. Correlates Mike Eisenberg's and Robert Berkowitz's
   Big6 Skills with the national Information Literacy Standards
   developed by the AASL and AECT and the National Educational
   Technology Standards for Students (NETS) to organize an introduction to research on the Internet.*

Big6 Newsletter *[Online]. Available: http://fp3e.adhost.com/big6/
   enewsletter/newsletter.shtml. Big6 Associates, Inc. publishes this
   newsletter four times a year.*

Collaborative   Planning   *[Online].   Available: http://es.
   houstonisd.org/ScrogginsES/information/library/collabor.html.
   This site includes the following: "Role of the Library Program in
   Information Literacy; A collaborative planning scenario; Clarifi-
   cation of the responsibility of the student, the teacher and the
   librarian in the collaboration process and a Sample project."*

Eisenberg, M. B. (1999). Essential skills for the information age:
   The Big6 in action *[Videotape]. Worthington, OH: Linworth.
   This video is a wonderful introduction to the Big6 model for all
   school personnel.*

Nuts and Bolts of the Big6 *[Online]. Available: http://www.kn.
   pacbell.com/wired/big6. This Web site states, "These days, everyone is talking about 'information literacy.' Along with the rapid
   deployment of technology came a glut of information. Information in and of itself has no meaning, but applied properly and in
   context, it is one of the most powerful tools of humankind. The
   problem is, how can we help students learn to separate the 'wheat
   from the chaff' and make good decisions about information? This
   is the crux of information literacy."*

The Seven Steps of the Research Process *[Online]. Available:
   http://www.library.cornell.edu/okuref/research/skill1.htm.
   According to Onlin and Uris Libraries, "The following seven
   steps outline a simple and effective strategy for finding information for a research paper and documenting the sources you
   find. Depending on your topic and your familiarity with the
   library, you may need to rearrange or recycle these steps. Adapt
   this outline to your needs." Try this out!*

Understanding How Teachers Plan: Strategies for Successful Instructional Partnerships *[Online]. Available: http://www. ala.org/cfapps/archive.cfm?path=aasl/SLMR/slmr_resources/sele ct_wolcott.html. Linda Wolcott explains, "Instructional consultation is a function that has been widely endorsed but not widely practiced."*

3

In the Classroom

INTRODUCTION

The first three information literacy standards for student learning as stated in *Information Power: Building Partnerships for Learning* (AASL & AECT, 1998) are as follows:

> *The student who is information literate accesses information efficiently and effectively.*
> *The student who is information literate evaluates information critically and competently.*
> *The student who is information literate uses information accurately and creatively.*

With these in mind, this chapter addresses accessing, evaluating, and using information. Remember, information is a commodity, and students who are most successful are those who can most efficiently access it, most critically evaluate and interpret it, and most effectively and ethically apply it. These are the fundamental skills of information literacy. Developing and reaching a level of independence and social responsibility to make appropriate use of that ability forms the substance of the information literacy standards for student learning. Information literacy is a process, and like other processes, it cannot be developed in isolation—it requires meaningful, authentic application.

To further clarify the critical nature of helping students become information literate in today's world, let's view some interesting statistics. Jones e-global library, a division of Jones Knowledge, Inc., commissioned a survey entitled *The Role of the Librarian in the Digital Age*. Surveys were sent to 10,000 randomly selected school library media specialists from institutions of various population sizes, geography, and funding; a statistically significant number were returned. Here are a few of the findings:

> When asked the question, "What are the most significant roles of the school library media specialist today?," 95% stated, "Instructing library users on the navigation and evaluation of print and digital information" and 94% declared, "Directing library users to appropriate information resources."
>
> When asked the question, "Do school library media specialists feel they currently have the skill of…directing library users to appropriate information resources," 90% remarked that they possess this skill. In addition, 86% believed that "they could instruct library users on the navigation and evaluation of print and digital information."
>
> When asked, "What will be the most significant roles of the school library media specialist in the next five years?," 92% stated, "Instructing library users on the navigation and evaluation of print and digital information." (2001)

This is wonderful news! Not only do school library media specialists believe that teaching information literacy skills is critically important, a majority of them feel equipped to deal with this important task. Furthermore, they believe that it will be of vital importance in the future. It appears that school library media specialists recognize what is important for students and are headed in the right direction. (For additional information regarding this survey, visit the following Web site: http://www.jonesknowledge.com/eglobal/ala_survey_school.html.)

On a less uplifting note, the Online Computer Library Center, Inc. (OCLC), commissioned a survey of U.S. college students to see how they use the Web for school-related assignments. The survey questioned 1,050 18–24 year old respondents representing all regions of the United States. This disturbing news about this survey is that only 4 percent of college students question the information they encounter (they believe that what is in black and white is truth). I wonder, what percentage of K–12 students question the information they encounter? (For more complete information regarding this survey, visit the following Web site: http://www2.oclc.org/oclc/pdf/printondemand/informationhabits.pdf, "OCLC White Paper on the Information Habits of College Students," June 2002).

ACCESSING

What exactly *is* access? Synonyms for access include such words as *open, retrieve, read,* and *logon.* This is precisely what information literate students should be able to do *with information.* However, what precisely *is* information? Are we talking about information the same way we did—say 30 years ago? Yes and no. Information is books, journals, pamphlets, magazines, newspapers, and so forth (as it was 30 years ago). However, today it is also online databases, CD-ROMs, Web sites, e-mail, listservs, and so forth—information is so much *more* than it was in the past. Think of it this way. A student comes into your school library media center and wants to know where to find information about gang violence. You have *numerous* places to retrieve (gain *access* to) information about gang violence. It is your responsibility (in part) to teach that student where and how to find information on this topic—this is all a part of the information literacy scene. A wide variety of formats are available: books, journals, magazines, newspapers, pamphlets, online databases, audiotapes, kits, videotapes, CD-ROMs, DVDs, laserdiscs, people, and so forth—and, of course, the millions of Web sites via the Internet. Yes, the school library media center contains mounds of information in-house and facilities to access information worldwide. So how, as a school library media specialist, do you begin to teach students where and how to access information efficiently and effectively and, once they've found the information, to evaluate and use it? Remember, to be information literate, a student accesses information competently and successfully—and *should* eventually become an independent, lifelong learner who uses problem-solving skills and critical thinking as part of their information-seeking knowledge. Wow! This is a big job, huh? And this is just *one small part* of information literacy in the twenty-first century.

According to the nine information literacy standards for student learning, accessing information includes the following indicators. The student who is information literate does the following:

> Recognizes the need for information;
> Recognizes that accurate and comprehensive information is the basis for intelligent decision-making;
> Formulates questions based on information needs;
> Identifies a variety of potential sources of information; and
> Develops and uses successful strategies for location information. (ALA, 1998, pp. 9–11)

Teaching these skills are *all* components of your job as a school library media specialist (in collaboration with the entire school community). Where does one begin? As Castro (2002) stated, "New [and former] students arrive at [school library media centers] every fall, thirsting for knowledge, but not bringing a cup. They encounter electronic databases, online catalogs, Web sites, multimedia—water, water everywhere, but no knowledge of how to drink. Without real information [literacy] skills, students searching for knowledge might as well be chasing a mirage in the desert" (p. 30).

Before assisting students' access to information, a reference/information literacy interview should occur, including the following:

What information does the student need?
What does the student already know about the subject?
Does the student have any preconceived ideas or biases on the topic?
What is the central focus of the student's information need?
How much information does the student need to gather?
What types of information does the student want?

Identifying the need—and teaching students to identify their *own* needs—is the first step to successful information access. To further clarify this, let's look at the following scenario.

You (Ms. Rahn) are a school library media specialist in a high school. Julie, a freshman student, is in need of information regarding home schooling for an upcoming English report:

Ms. Rahn: Hi Julie, what can I do for you today?

Julie: Hi Ms. Rahn. I need to find some information about home schooling for an English report that is due in two weeks.

Ms. Rahn: Can you tell me more about what you need?

Julie: We are just supposed to write a report about some aspect of schools and learning for my English class. I thought it would be interesting to write about home schooling.

Ms. Rahn: Good idea, Julie. Have you gotten any background information about the topic already?

Julie: No, not really. But I do have a friend who is home schooled.

Ms. Rahn: Great! I'll bet you've learned lots about this topic from your friend. Is there anything specific that you want to write about concerning home schooling?

Julie: Well, kind of. My friend talks about how lonely she is sometimes. I would like to know if other kids being home schooled feel the same way. Gosh, I think I would be lonely without school—and activities and friends.

Ms. Rahn: Sounds like a wonderful idea! How much information do you need for your report?

Julie: It is supposed to be about 10 pages long—double-spaced, of course!

Ms. Rahn: Fine. Do you need a variety of formats—such as books and journal articles and Web sites?

Julie: My teacher said we could use any source as long as we put it in the bibliography—and use a minimum of three resources…and to give credit to the people—well, you know, not plagiarize.

Ms. Rahn: Exactly! Your teacher is right. Julie, one resource is your friend—you might want to talk with her—interview your friend about being home schooled (if that is ok with her and her parents). Since home schooling is a rather hot topic, I think we should begin with books and then look at recent journal articles and Web sites. What do you think?

Julie: I agree. That sounds great! I know my friend and her parents won't mind if I talk to her. They are really nice people. What journals should I look at?... and I am not sure where to begin on the Internet.

Ms. Rahn: That's fine. We will learn now. I will show you how to use the online databases EBSCO and SIRS to locate your journal articles and then we will talk about how to use search words—and the appropriate search engines and subject directories to find just the information you need on the Internet. From these resources, you should be able to come up with a variety of pertinent questions to ask your friend about home schooling.

Julie: This is awesome! I can't wait. I have over an hour before I have to be home.

Ms. Rahn: Good, Julie. Let's get right to work. I feel certain that I can teach you the basics about online databases and search terms in that amount of time, and you can take it from there. I also have a handout I can give you about online databases, search engines, subject directories, and keyword searching.

Julie: Thanks so much, Ms. Rahn. You're the best!

What occurred in this scenario? The school library media specialist began to teach a student one basic information literacy skill, access to information. It's not as difficult as you thought, right? Teaching information literacy skills begins with good communication skills. Communication with your students is the key to success—whether it is ready reference questions or policies and procedures. As stated by Riedling (2000b), "The effective [information literacy interview] takes practice and creativity; it efficiently connects knowledge with the student's information needs. It is critical that school library media specialists learn to listen and communicate with students effectively... it is virtually impossible to divorce human relations from communications skills. It is vital to remember that [you] are... bringing students and information together. It is up to [you] to ensure that everything possible is done to keep the channels of communication open and flowing. As important as library media specialists are to students, students are even more important to librarians, for they are the lifeblood of the profession" (p. 89).

So far, Julie is learning or knows (along with the assistance of the school library media specialist):

How to recognize the need for information (her English report about home schooling)
That accurate and comprehensive information is the basis for intelligent decision making (interviewing people, accessing current, relevant information)
How to formulate questions based on information needs (learning about home schooling to intelligently interview her friend)
How to identify a variety of potential sources of information (online databases, Web sites, etc.)
How to develop and use successful strategies for locating information (search engines, subject directories, keyword searching, and so forth)

These are the basic standards and indicators of information access as expressed in *Information Power: Building Partnerships for Learning* (AASL & AECT, 1998).

A useful and organized method for students to learn to access information effectively and efficiently is via handouts. The school library media specialist can easily provide these. The purpose is to encourage students to form the appropriate questions and focus for locating their needed information. Castro (2002) explains one example of an outline. The core competencies are as follows:

State a research question, problem or issue
Locate and retrieve relevant information
Organize information
Analyze information
Synthesize information
Communicate using a variety of information technologies
Use the technological tools for accessing information. (p. 31)

This describes an overall organizational plan for retrieving information. It may also be helpful for students to complete a handout similar to the following:

State your assignment topic.

Write the name of one resource that you could use to help you understand your assignment topic.

Create a search plan. From your assignment topic, write out at least three concepts of the topic along with their alternative keywords:

Keywords for Concept 1:
Keywords for Concept 2:
Keywords for Concept 3:

List the types and formats of information sources you will need for your assignment.
Locate and access your information sources—and obtain them.

Students are born learners, constantly reacting to the world around them and trying to make sense of it. Today's students are surrounded by technology in every form. Sometimes that technology provides information, but it can be used to manipulate and distort information. Therefore, students need explicit instruction on ways to access and *evaluate* the technology-generated messages that bombard them daily. Fortunately, school library media specialists can use their knowledge of information literacy processes to help students find order and meaning in their surroundings. The following section will discuss evaluation of information resources—a vital component of information literacy.

The following is an example of how to teach evaluation of Web sites:

KATHY SCHROCK'S INTERNET CURRICULUM
CRITICAL EVALUATION OF A WEB PAGE
LESSON PLAN: GRADES 6–8

ESSENTIAL QUESTION

Why is it important to evaluate the source and validity of the information found on a Web site?

NETS'S STANDARD AND PERFORMANCE INDICATOR

Technology Research Tools

Students use technology to locate, evaluate and collect information from a variety of sources.

Research and evaluate the accuracy, relevance, appropriateness, comprehensiveness, and bias of electronic information sources concerning real world problems.

MATERIALS

Inspiration®, computer, and projection device (or overhead and brainstorming transparency)

Critical evaluation tool for each student

Internet access or hard copy of Web page for each student

5 W's handout for each student

The Important Book summarizer sheet

PROCEDURE

Using Inspiration® and the computer (or the overhead and the *transparency*), have the students brainstorm a list of criteria which make a Web page useful for research. Answers should include title, author, date of creation, date of update, source of information, contact e-mail address, layout of page, ease of use, fast to load, etc.

Hand out the *5 W's handout* and the *Critical Evaluation Tool* and go over both. Be sure to emphasize the importance of the credibility of the author and the source of the information on the page. Talk about ways to determine if information is correct (e.g., finding the information in a print source, on another Web page, via an expert)

Surf to the Ban Dihydrogen Monoxide page (http://ddescy.lme.mnsu.edu/descy/webcred/webcred/dhmo.html) or hand out the *PDF version* and have students, on their own or in small groups, evaluate the information on the page using the critical evaluation tool.

Have the class come back as a group and discuss the pro's and con's of this page. Did anyone know the information was bogus? How could this be determined? Emphasize the fact, with little knowledge of a topic, it is almost impossible to know if the information located is correct.

In small groups, have students visit some of the other bogus Web sites listed at the bottom of this page:
http://discoveryschool.com/schrock guide/eval.html
Have them discuss the methods for finding out if the information is real or bogus.

ASSESSMENT

Have the students fill out *The Important Book Summarizing Sheet*.
Have the students write a paragraph explaining why it is important to evaluate the information found on a Web page. Have them include the ways to find out more about the author, the sponsoring agency, or the information itself.
Have the students create a list of 10 questions to ask themselves when critically evaluating the information they have found.

EXTENSION ACTIVITIES

1. Have students write a one-page instruction sheet for younger students explaining the Web page evaluation process.
2. Have students identify other Web sites dealing with critical evaluation of Web information and create a Web page with links and descriptions of the sites.

EVALUATING

As stated in *Information Power: Building Partnerships for Learning* (AASL & AECT, 1998),

> The student who is information literate... understands traditional and emerging principles for assessing the accuracy, validity, relevance, completeness and impartiality of information. The student applies these principles insightfully across information sources and formats and uses logic and informed judgment to accept, reject, or replace information to meet a particular need.

> [*Information literate students must be able to:*]
>
> *Determine accuracy, relevance, and comprehensiveness;*
> *Distinguish among fact, point of view, and opinion;*
> *Identify inaccurate and misleading information; and*
> *Select information appropriate to the problem or question at hand.*
>
> (*pp. 14–15*)

As Riedling (2002) stated,

> Print, nonprint, and Web-based resources offer [students] the opportunity to locate information and data from all over the world. However, finding appropriate, thought-provoking materials...requires time and expertise. It is vital to evaluate all sources, identifying the most suitable ones.... Today there is a myriad of information and resources available via the Internet. This is good news and bad news. The good news is that so much more information is readily accessible, and the bad news is that much more of it is inadequate. Thus, it is [the school library media specialist's] responsibility to develop expertise in evaluating the information...required...[and teach this skill to your students]. (p. 63)

We need to recognize that school library media specialists have been teaching students to look at authority, reliability (evaluation) of print—and even nonprint—resources for years. School library media specialists and teachers carefully select books and other print and nonprint materials that students regularly use. Students *assume* that print and nonprint resources in the school library media center are appropriate, factual, and reliable because the school library media specialists (and others) have evaluated them before students view them—students sense little need to think about these items as anything but the truth. Students have limited experience with false, erroneous, or strongly biased information. When it comes to computers and the World Wide Web, students can be quite naïve. They believe that someone patrols the Internet—because they are used to having factual information presented to them—and nothing but! Herein lays a problem. We now have the Internet that, in addition to being extremely accessible by any student, can contain information written by literally anyone—*it has not been evaluated before student use!* Let's, face it, the Internet is a terrific information resource; however, it can often be confusing and frustrating—along with providing *mis*information. Therefore, there has become an urgency to teach students (and others) how to evaluate Web-based resources. As teachers and administrators become aware of the immense amount of resources on the Web, they also realize the vital role school library media specialists play in helping students (and teachers) become information literate in an electronic information world.

When evaluating Web-based resources, we must teach students to ask the right questions. What are those questions? The following are examples:

How is the Web-based resource different from other materials?
Is the information on the Web more comprehensive or timely than those of traditional resources?
Will the Web-based resource contribute to deeper understanding of content or concepts?
What is the purpose of the Web site?
Who owns the Web site and why?
Who is the author or creator of the information?
Is the information accurate and reliable?
How recent is the information?
Is the information well written and grammatically correct?
Does the site contain links to other sites that are useful—and unbiased?
Does the Web site function efficiently?
Does the site incorporate the unique capabilities of the World Wide Web?
Is the information meaningful and useful for your research?

As school library media specialists, you must look at this in a positive manner. YOU have the *unique* opportunity to take a *leadership role* in teaching students, teachers, and others all about the Internet!

Let's look at Web site evaluation more practically. As discussed previously, information comes in a wide variety of formats (print, nonprint,

Web-based, and so forth). Evaluation of information remains basically the same for all formats, although evaluation of some formats can be more difficult than others. For example, it is rather simple to determine the author, publisher, and publication date of a print resource. It is typically located on the verso page (behind the title page) in a book. Author and publishing information for nonprint materials are typically included in descriptive ancillary materials or within the source itself. However, locating the author, publisher and publication of a *Web site* can be a bit more difficult. Where is this information located on a Web site? To answer this question—and many more—it is helpful to use specific criteria to assist you—and your students—with the evaluation of print, nonprint, and Web-based materials.

The following four criteria are merely one set of criteria; numerous variations have been published and can be extremely useful:

Accuracy and authority
Objectivity
Currency
Scope

Accuracy and authority involve the education and experience of the creators, editors, and contributors of information, as well as the reputation of the publisher or sponsoring agency. Typically, accuracy and authority of print resources have been predetermined by reviewers (that you, as a school library media specialist, have then reviewed via selection and evaluation tools). In other words, those who created, edited, or published the resource were screened and selected based on factual reviews (that you reviewed for appropriateness in your school library media center). That makes it quite simple for a print source—students need not worry about evaluation of this format (in general). The authors (creators) are usually provided, along with their credentials. The same holds true for the editors and publishers of the material. This is also the case for *nonprint* materials (such as videotapes, CD-ROMs, DVDs, kits, and so forth). The same basic criteria apply, although it may be a bit trickier to discover. You may need to preview the resources or look in descriptive ancillary materials. Again, students trust your evaluation of these resources *because they are in your school library media center.*

Determining accuracy and authority of *Web-based materials* can be even more challenging. Remember, anyone with the right software and access to the Internet can publish a document on the Web, regardless of accuracy or quality of presentation. You (and your students), along with the assistance of others and experts, and by comparing the resource to other similar information, should be able to measure accuracy appropriately. An accurate piece of information will include an impartial presentation of information and balanced representations of cultural, ethnic, and racial groups. The author or creator of a Web site should be clearly visible on the site—along with an e-mail address. Typically, this information is found at the bottom portion of the home page. Now you know who the author or creator is—but are they qualified to write this work? What is the purpose of this document and why was it produced? Authoritative works *should* include the creator's credentials. If they are not included, you should research the creator. Look elsewhere on the Web, ask experts in the field, look at print and nonprint resources, and so on. One last resort is to type the name of the creator in www.google.com (using quotation marks); this will bring up any previous information by or about the creator. To determine authority of a Web-based resource, you should also check the domain of the document and what institution publishes it (for example, if it is ".gov,"the site is more likely to be accurate and authoritative). These can all be easily executed by students as well—*teach them!*

Now let's look at *objectivity* of resources. What is objectivity? This includes coverage of the topics that provides factual, unbiased information. Does the author have biases? How reliable are the facts presented? Typically, *print and nonprint* materials include a statement of purpose (in the prefatory or ancillary information) that helps clarify objectivity—so we will not elaborate, as students (once again!) trust your wonderful, accurate decisions about the materials they locate and use in your school library media center.

With *Web-based* sources, objectivity is again more difficult to determine. However, as with print and nonprint materials, the same items should be viewed and the same questions asked. For instance, let's assume that you (your student) are attempting to discern the objectivity of a Web site regarding abortion. We are all aware that there are two sides to the abortion issue. Can you tell by viewing the Web site whether it is pro or con? Who created or published the site? What is the purpose of this Web site; is it obvious? Does it contain facts? If so, attempt to locate the facts in another source to see if they match. Does the Web site include loaded words? Are the comments disparaging? Are the illustrations balanced? What is the date on this Web site and has it been recently updated? Determining objectivity may take time, but the results will be worth the effort. It may be helpful to present a worksheet checklist students can use when determining objectivity. It is your responsibility as a school library media specialist to offer materials in all formats that are objective. *It is also your responsibility to assist students to do the same—to become information literate.*

The following is an example of a lesson plan demonstrating how to detect bias in Web sites.

EVALUATING WEB SITES FOR BIAS

Subjects: Arts & Humanities, Educational Technology, Holidays, Language Arts, Social Studies, U.S. History
Grades: 6–8, 9–12, Advanced

Brief Description

Students use a checklist to evaluate Web content about Martin Luther King Jr. for bias.

Objectives

Students use the checklist to evaluate two Web sites from very different sources.
Students become familiar with the checklist they use to evaluate Web content for bias.

Keywords

evaluate, Martin Luther King, media literacy, Web literacy, Web sites

Materials Needed

Internet access (preferred over printing and distributing Web content)
Checklist for Evaluating Web Resources at http://library.usm.maine. edu/guides/webeval.html

Lesson Plan

In this activity, pairs of students visit two Web sites about Martin Luther King Jr. and evaluate the content and credibility. Students use a checklist that will guide them as they consider the sponsor of each Web site, the validity of the information presented, evidence of bias, and so on.
See the Web Team Developers Guide lesson plan at http://gateways. unhny.org/LESWT/savvy.phtml. Click on Evaluation Activity 1

Assessment

Lesson Plan Source

The American Gateways/Settlement House Initiative.

National Standards

Language Arts

English
Grades K–12
NL-ENG.K-12.1 Reading for Perspective
NL-ENG.K-12.2 Reading for Understanding
NL-ENG.K-12.3 Evaluation Strategies
NL-ENG.K-12.8 Developing Research Skills

Social Sciences

U.S. History
Grades 5–12
NSS-USH.5–12.9 Era 9: Postwar United States (1945 to early 1970s)
NSS-USH.5–12.10 Era 10: Contemporary United States (1968 To The Present)

Technology

Grades K–12
NT.K-12.1 Basic Operations and Concepts
NT.K-12.2 Social, Ethical, and Human Issues
NT.K-12.5 Technology Research Tools

Currency of *print, nonprint,* and *Web-based* materials is much easier to establish. Print materials typically have a copyright date located on the page behind the title page. Likewise, newspapers and periodicals usually include a date of publication. Nonprint resources also characteristically have a copyright date either in the descriptive ancillary materials or noted within the item itself (for example, a CD-ROM may have the date on the outer package or on the first page, when opening it on the computer). Currency is vitally important, particularly in specific areas such as medicine, technology, geography, and so forth. If you cannot locate a copyright date, view the source to see if you can determine a time frame. Your students assume you know this and have selected the best and most current print and nonprint resources available!

Web-based sources should include a date (possibly a date created and a date of last revision). If no date obviously appears, look for policy statements on information maintenance and link maintenance. By viewing links to a Web site, clues may be given regarding the date of creation. Remember, however, that there is no guarantee that a particular site will reside in the same location today as it did yesterday. If you locate a good or useful Web site, write down the date and time you visited it *(and teach your students to do the same)*. Students can easily learn to observe the signs of Web-based currency. Review this with them, provide a worksheet, and assist them as needed.

Scope of a material refers to the basic breadth-and-depth question—What is covered and in what detail? It should reflect the purpose of the source and its intended audience. Aspects of scope include subject, geographic location, and time period. *Print and nonprint* resources usually include the scope in the statement of purpose, which is often found in the preface, introduction, or accompanying ancillary materials.

For *Web-based* resources, look for the stated purpose on the Web site, along with any limitations that may apply and any comments on the site's comprehensiveness. A good Web site should boldly explain what is covered and in what detail. It is important to determine if a source has accomplished what it intended. *Even more important is that you teach your students to do the same—to become independent, lifelong learners.* Now you (and your students) have accessed information and evaluated it. It is time to look at how information is used.

USING

As stated in *Information Power: Building Partnerships for Learning* (AASL & AECT, 1998),

The student who is information literate...manages information skillfully and effectively in a variety of contexts. That student organizes and integrates information from a range of sources and formats in order to apply it to decision-making, problem solving, critical thinking and creative expression. Rather than suggesting that students simply insert researched information into a perfunctory product...students use information to draw conclusions and develop new understandings by:

> *Organizing information for practical application;*
> *Integrating new information into one's own knowledge;*
> *Applying information in critical thinking and problem solving; and*
> *Producing and communicating information and ideas in appropriate formats.*
>
> (pp. 19–20)

How do students learn to *organize* Web-based information? How, as a school library media specialist, do you teach this skill? What is organization of information? Actually, this is not a new concept. Organizing research has been done for many, many years. However, organizing *today's* information is somewhat more complex than in the past. Several of the critical thinking/problem-solving models regarding organization of information were described in chapter 2. These models provide excellent templates for orderliness of information (see chapter 2). For example, as a school library media specialist, you might suggest to a student to think about or write down the following before or while researching regarding organization:

Task/problem (assignment/reason for need of information)
Search strategy (choose, narrow, plan, locate, analyze, evaluate, etc.)
Organization of notes (e.g., chronologically, topically, hierarchically)

Focus Question (central theme of topic chosen)
Sources of information (Internet, print resources, people, etc.)
Keywords (synonyms and expansions of topic words)

"Students organize information to make sense of it and to present it most effectively to others. They understand their intended audience, the demands of the presentation format, and the essential ideas in the topic or issue being presented" (ALA, 1998, p. 19). *This is a school library media specialist's goal!*

Organizing information is a daily activity for most of us. We continually group similar things together, put things into categories, and so forth. Information organization is an essential ingredient of our existence because of the sea of unstructured information we live in today.

Visual learning techniques are graphic ways of working with ideas and presenting information to teach students to clarify their thinking and to process, organize, and prioritize new information. Visual diagrams reveal patterns, interrelationships, and interdependencies. They also stimulate creative thinking.

The following are examples of graphic organizers. (To obtain further information about each, please visit: www.sdcoe.K12.ca.us/score/actbank/sorganize.htm.)

Chain of Events
Clustering
Compare/Contrast
Continuum
Cycle
Family Tree
Fishbone
Interaction Outline
Problem/Solution
Spider
Storyboard
Venn Diagram

One significant and well-used graphic organizer in today's K–12 environment is the software *Inspiration®*. This software package supports critical thinking, comprehension, and writing in all curriculum areas. (*Kidspiration* is typically used for primary grades). The Web also offers a wonderful list of printable graphic organizers, which can be found at www.teachervision.fen.com/lesson-plans/lesson-6293.htm. Yet another Web site, which provides an overview of webbing, concept mapping, matrix, and flow chart is located at: www.graphic.org/goindex.html.

How does a student *integrate* Web-based information? Integration of information is based on a student's current knowledge. It is important to teach students to recognize and understand new information, draw conclusions regarding the "old and new" information, and integrate knowledge previously acquired from a variety of sources to create new meaning (print, nonprint, Web-based materials). Let's look at a concrete example. Your student (11th grade) is researching violence in schools for a class paper. The student has done some prior research (reading, talking to others, etc.), but locates several new online articles and Web sites about school violence. The student is able to recall what he/she previously knew and integrates it with the new/current information to create a *new meaning*. As a school library media specialist, are you capable of assisting students with integration (previous and current knowledge) of information? Help your students to recall what they know and integrate that information within the new information retrieved. A suggested activity is as follows:

> Outline what they know: who, what where, when, why—and how that information was obtained.
> Locate preliminary background information.
> Use the library—online databases, print resources, indexes, and so forth.
> Locate desired information on the Internet (using Web evaluation skills).
> Look for information in other formats—CD-ROMs, DVDs, videotapes, and so forth.
> Cite what is found and where it was found.
> Work from the general to the specific.
> Don't forget obvious assistance—dictionaries, thesauri, and people!

How does a student (how do you *teach* a student to) *apply* information in critical thinking and problem-solving? An eighth-grade student,

Bob, is looking for information concerning the Gulf War. He views some print and nonprint materials and finds basic information about this war. Then Bob searches the Internet and finds *numerous* sites regarding the Gulf War. He not only identifies the new information and uses it to answer a question, but he devises creative approaches for using this information to resolve the problem/question at hand. For example, Bob creates a "military plan" to use in the Gulf War based on information he located about military plans in World War II. He has learned to *apply* information. As a school library media specialist, how do you teach this skill?

Principle learning skills consist of being able to formulate a question, accessing resources of information, evaluating the information, organizing the information and applying the information to answer the question. This last competency could be considered the most important step in the learning process because it is not simply the finding of information, but the use of it that motivates the learner. A number of national reports emphasize the centrality of information literacy in the learning process (Doyle, 1994).

Students need to know how to arrange and document their research appropriately. For example, stress the need for consistency in citing sources and specify a style manual (APA, MLA, Turabian, etc.) to be used. Discussion of copyright and plagiarism is also desirable.

Students need to know how to critically assess the results of their research to determine appropriateness of their methods and findings for their class assignment. After their assessment, the student can make needed corrections to their research. For example, if the class assignment is a term paper, break it into manageable parts by constructing a series of assignments with due dates. This helps students structure the term paper process and learn from each step:

Identifying a topic from a list of choices
After discussion of criteria (resources to use), gathering of sources
Preparing an annotated bibliography
Developing an outline of paper (title and major points)
Writing a first draft including citing of sources
Rewriting
Turning in term paper

> *Due to the large amount of information available to easily cut and paste, it is becoming increasingly difficult for students to determine how to effectively cite sources or even give credit to original creators of information. For this reason, an emphasis on using information has become one of the major tenants of information competency. Finding information is only half of the battle. Information literate students must be aware of copyright issues as well as proper citation styles or methods for every information type they use.*
>
> *(Granted with permission from: http://www.csulb.edu/~ttravis/IC/CSULB/applyinfo.htm. Tutorial created by Suan Luévano, Eileen Wakiji, and Tiffini Travis.)*

This involves your knowing what information Bob knows and needs (reference interview) and how to assist him in using a variety of resources and approaches to answer his question. Communication is key. To bring Bob from reading to application requires knowledge of resources and presentation options. As a school library media specialist, you are the passage from resources to application.

Students need to then *produce and communicate* information in acceptable formats. Again, how does a school library media specialist teach students to accomplish this? First, it is highly unlikely that students have been taught that there *are* numerous ways to present information. For many students, research presentation = research paper. However, it is important that students understand that various kinds of information are better presented in a particular format. Let's look at this practically.

Amy, a fifth-grade student, has researched a variety of sources concerning penguins. She has compiled the information and is to present this to her class. Amy realizes that it would be more interesting and meaningful if her classmates could see pictures of penguins, their habitat, the foods they eat, how they react with one another, and so forth. She believes that creating a PowerPoint presentation with these types of pictures, along with the information, would get the information across in a more interesting and thought provoking manner. Amy asks her teacher and the school library media specialist about the possibility of showing a PowerPoint presentation in her class-

room. The school library media center houses a portable projector that can be moved from room to room. Amy's teacher agrees that the classroom is large enough and the seats can be arranged such that everyone can see her presentation. After one-on-one instruction by the library media specialist regarding PowerPoint techniques and strategies, Amy produces a PowerPoint presentation and shows it to the class. It is a huge success!

In this scenario, Amy has learned to present and communicate her information in the most appropriate format. She understands that visuals will enhance the presentation because of its content and has thought about her audience (classmates) and how this can be accomplished in her classroom. Amy has learned to "produce and communicate information and ideas in appropriate formats" (ALA, 1998, p. 20).

Using information accurately and creatively is just as much a part of being information literate as is evaluating information. It is *your* job, as school library media specialist, (along with other school personnel) to instill these skills in young people. *No one said it would be easy, but wouldn't it be wonderful to produce information literate, independent, lifelong learners—what an accomplishment!*

RESEARCH AND DEVELOPMENT

Our technological age has forced school library media specialists to reexamine the role that they play in the teaching and learning process. The technological age has also encouraged them to expand their vision to include new programs and new solutions. As Castro (2002) stated, "Students encounter vast quantities of electronic information, but they don't really know how to drink it all in" (p. 30). She continues by asking, "How do you take those thousands of fresh, new faces and help them to understand when they need information, where to look, and how to evaluate what they find—in short, how do you teach them to become information literate? Integrating information skills into every class across the curriculum is the way to go..." (p. 30). Callison (2001) remarks, "In the context of student learning through information literacy, there is a need to give more attention than has been provided previously to strategies for understanding information and how to use what is extracted in a meaningful and constructive way" (p. 32). As school library media specialists, you must become leaders—pioneers in teaching information access, evaluation, and use. Todd (1999) remarks, "Transformational leadership and learning are all about creating and providing opportunities for learners to make the most of their life opportunities in a world rich in information and technology. Developing teaching strategies to address these skills, however, is a complex, time-consuming and challenging process" (p. 4). By now, school library media specialists should be accustomed to challenges because they are a part of the everyday work world. Therefore, the challenge of leadership regarding information literacy must not frighten you, but should appear as *a unique opportunity* (as stated earlier in this chapter) to help students (and others in the school community) make sense out of the deluge of information at everyone's fingertips—and in everyone's lives. Todd continues by saying, "Improved learning outcomes through information [literacy] do not happen by chance. For students to be connected to information [literacy], transformed by it, empowered through it, and to use it in their lives requires educational intervention that is thoughtfully conceived and implemented. This demands visionary leadership..." (p. 5). A school library media specialist must have *the vision*—but not only that, he or she must have a plan (guided activities) for teaching information literacy skills and the power to apply them. Troutner (2002) has written an extremely useful article to assist school library media specialists in teaching information literacy skills. Actually, this resource consists of numerous Web sites that deal with research, search strategies, and so forth. Do not feel alone in this information literacy endeavor. An unbelievable amount of materials are available to assist you (print, nonprint, and Web-based) so that you do not have to re-create the wheel.

The following books, articles, and Web sites are useful and thought-provoking information that should make your job easier as a leader in information literacy education. Keep in mind that you are *not alone*. Thousands of school library media specialists are addressing these same types of issues. Read, explore Web sites, talk to colleagues, and attend conferences and workshops. All of these will make your *new role* much easier to comprehend, apply, and appreciate.

PRINT

Bucher, K. T. (2000). The importance of information literacy skills in the middle school curriculum. Clearing House, 73(4), 217–220. *The author of this article contends that information literacy or library skills are ignored in the middle school curriculum.*

Calishain, T. (2002). Yahoo! Service offers more advice than expertise. Information Today, 19(6), 51. *This article evaluates the Yahoo! Advice search engine, including features of the services, similarity to others, and so forth.*

Clyde, A. (2002). The invisible web. Teacher Librarian, 29(4), 47–50. *This article examines the concept of the invisible web and describes features, uses, and so forth.*

Cooke, A. (1999). Authoritative guide to evaluating information on the Internet. *New York: Neal-Schuman. This book provides an empirical method for eliminating misinformation and time-wasting sites from the selection process.*

Drabenstott, K. M. (2001). Web search strategy development. Online, 25(4), 18–27. *This article examines Web searching tools and discusses new searching strategies.*

Ercoegovac, Z. (2001). Information literacy: Search strategies, tools, and resources for high school students. *Worthington, OH: Linworth. This book takes a student-centered perspective, draws on learning theories, and offers a tested program.*

Farmer, L. S. J. (2001). Getting an early start on using technology for research. Library Talk, 15(2), 24–26. *This article discusses ways of helping students use computer technology to conduct effective research.*

Goldsborough, R. (2002). Can the Internet be trusted? Reading Today, 19(4), 15. *This article presents a reminder to teachers and students concerning the use of the Internet.*

Grimes, B. (2002). Expand your Web search horizons. PC World, 20(6), 53–54. *This article provides information on several search engines and information that can be found using different search tools.*

Haycock, K., Dober, M., & Edwards, B. (2003). The Neal-Schuman authoritative guide to kids' search engines, subject directories, and portals. *New York: Neal-Schuman. Based on recent research and a review of the literature, this book explains children's search-ing behaviors and describes the types of logical thinking, critical evaluation, and search strategies needed when conducting research on the Web.*

Jacobson, T. E., & Xu, L. (2004). Motivating students in informa-tion literacy classes. *New York: Neal-Schuman. This book shows librarians and instructors how to develop engaging courses that will compel students to become effective and efficient users of information.*

Jones, C. (2001). *Infusing information literacy and technology into your school library media program.* Knowledge Quest, 30(1), 32–33. *This article focuses on infusing technology and instruc-tional strategies into a school library media program aimed at K–5 students.*

Kubly, K. (1997). *Guiding students in using the World Wide Web for research.* Mid-South Instructional Technology Conference Pro-ceedings. *Murfreesboro, TN, April 8–9, 1997. This paper addresses the need for educators and librarians to guide students in using the World Wide Web appropriately by teaching them to evaluate Internet resources using criteria designed to identify the authoritative sources.*

Langford, L. (2001). *A building block towards the information literate school community.* Teacher Librarian, 28(5), 18–21. *In this article, the author states, "Industrial Age schooling must crumble and give rise to a more student-centered, goal-oriented, caring environ-ment...."*

McLaughlin, L., & Spring, T. (2004). *The straight story on search engines.* PC World, 20(7), 115–124. *This article discusses Internet search engines, effectiveness of their searches, and the technology that they use.*

Minkel, W. (1997). *Lost (& found) in cyberspace.* School Library Journal, 43(3), 102–105. *This article examines how to make search engines work for you.*

O'Sullivan, M., & Scott, T. (2000). *Teaching Internet information literacy: A critical evaluation.* Multimedia Schools, 7(2), 40–44. *This article discusses the idea that the Internet is a valuable research tool, but many students need guidance on refining their searches.*

Pierson, M. (1997). The honeymoon is over. Technology Connection, *4(4), 10. This article presents guidelines for leading students toward productive Internet searches.*

Pooley, P., & Pooley, E. (2001, March). 7 steps to smarter Web searches. Family Life, *31–33. This article provides seven easy-to-follow steps to searching the World Wide Web.*

Smith, C. B. (2001). Getting to know the invisible web. Library Journal, *126(11), 16–18. This article reveals how to get at the Internet's hidden resources.*

Valenza, J. K. (1997). Master the art of searching. Electronic Learning, *16(5), 62. This article provides information relevant to Internet searching.*

Weinstein, C. E., Ridley, D. S., Dahl, T., & Weber, E. S. (1989). Helping students develop strategies for effective learning. Educational Leadership, *46(4), 17–19. This article discusses elaboration strategies—creating analogies, paraphrasing and summarizing—for long-term retention by students.*

Wildstrom, S. H. (1995). Feeling your way around the web. Business Week, *3441, 22. This article suggests ways of exploring Web sites, the use of various search tools, index tools, and so forth.*

NONPRINT

Guide to WWW Research: Web Page Types *[Online]. Available: http://www.slu.edu/departments/english/research/page3.html. A quote from this Web site explains, "While the information presented in advocacy pages is slanted by definition, advocates are often the only people who care enough about particular issues to thoroughly investigate them."*

Jungwirth, B., & Bruce, B. C. (2002). Information overload: Threat or opportunity? Reading Online *[Online]. Available: http://readingonline.org. This article deals with the question, "Do we really have to deal with an information overload, or are the developments in telecommunications just a great opportunity to become better informed?"*

Learning More about Search Engines and Subject Directories: FAQs *[Online]. Available: http://www.cln.org/searching_faqs.*

html. *This extremely informative Web site provides a set of FAQs on how to use Internet Search Engines and Subject Directories.*

Online Writing Lab (OWL) *[Online]. Available: http://owl.english. purdue.edu. This useful Web site includes tutorials, a grammar hotline, a collection of references material, and much more.*

Smith, Alastair. Evaluation of Information Sources *[Online]. Available: http://www.vuw.ac.nz/~agsmith/evaln/evaln.htm. This page contains pointers to criteria for evaluating information resources, particularly those on the Internet. It is intended to be particularly useful to school librarians and others who are selecting sites to include in an information resource guide, or informing users of the qualities they should use in evaluating Internet information.*

Subject Directories *[Online]. Available: http://www.lib. berkeley.edu/TeachingLib/Guides/Internet/SubjDirectories.html. This Web site provides general subject directories (tables of contents) for Librarians' Index, Infomine, Academic Info, About.com, and Yahoo.*

Sullivan, D. Boolean Searching *[Online]. Available: http://www. searchenginewatch.com/facts/boolean.html. This site discusses the following: "Boolean search commands have been used by professionals for searching through traditional databases for years. Despite this, they are overkill for the average web user."*

Sullivan, D. Power Searching for Anyone *[Online]. Available: http://www.searchenginewatch.com/facts/powersearch.html. "Search engines have a variety of ways for you to refine and control your searches. Some of them offer menu systems for this. Others require you to use special commands as part of your query."*

Web Awareness: The 5 Ws (and 1 H) of Cyberspace *[Online]. Available: http://www.media-awareness.ca/eng/webaware/tipsheets/w5.htm. This site offers resources and support for those interested in media and information literacy for young people.*

4

In Your Mind

INTRODUCTION

The Independent Learning Standards 4, 5, and 6, as explained in *Information Power: Building Partnerships for Learning,* are as follows:

> *The student who is an independent learner is information literate and pursues information related to personal interests.*
>
> *The student who is an independent learner is information literate and appreciates literature and other creative expressions of information.*
>
> *The student who is an independent learner is information literate and strives for excellence in information seeking and knowledge generation. (AASL & AECT, 1998, pp. 23–29)*

Knowledge seeking is not just a classroom experience. We seek information practically every day of our lives. What medicine should I take for a sinus headache? Where can I purchase the least expensive computer monitor? Should I buy a new car now; if so, what kind? Where should we go on vacation this summer? All of these require information literacy skills. As a student, these will vary, such as What college should I attend? What would my friend like for graduation? How can I send an online birthday card? What is the fastest route to the movie theatre? *Information Power* states, "The student constructs meaningful personal knowledge based on...information...[and] seeks information related to various dimensions of personal well-being, such as career interests, community involvement, health matters, and recreational pursuits" (p. 23).

INDEPENDENT LEARNING

Information literacy encompasses not only facts but leisure materials as well. According to *Information Power,* "The student who is an independent learner applies the principles of information literacy to access, evaluate, enjoy, value, and create artistic products" (ALA, 1998, p. 26). It takes knowledge to evaluate a work of fiction or a work of art—and to enjoy and value it. These skills can also be taught and learned. *Information Power* states, "[A] student [who is an independent learner] actively and independently reflects on and critiques personal thought processes and individually created information products" (p. 29). *Reflection* is a key word here. Students must learn to reflect so they can understand what is good and bad, revise, improve, and update. According to Rafoth (2001), in *Inspiring Independent Learning,* "Successful students know how to study, prepare for exams, identify important information in teacher talk and monitor their own learning" (p. 60). Fostering independent learning is a necessary skill for students—and can be taught by using a variety of activities and strategies. Again, this is yet *one more job* for the school library media specialist!

RESEARCH AND DEVELOPMENT

Actually, a minimal amount of research is available regarding independent learning and information literacy. However, I believe that it is a critical characteristic of a student who will be committed to lifelong learning, make independent decisions by using informed opinions, and find pleasure in the creative arts. Pappas (2002) remarks, "So the question arises, how do we teach the appreciation of other media?...Appreciation involves developing an understanding of a medium and learning how artists and writers construct meaning within that medium...Young people today are living in a visual world and need to learn to convey ideas in a visual format" (p. 25). Rankin (1996) says, "It is no accident that visual displays have become increasingly common in an information-rich world. They attract our attention more readily than blocks of text. They summarize and organize data" (p. 148). Pappas explains, "Appreciation is more than just understanding how a creative work is constructed. Appreciation also is related to our personal values system...Students may need many opportunities to develop their own value system related to different forms of creative expression. As educators, we need to give them those opportunities" (2002, p. 26).

Students need to appreciate a variety of types of information: by viewing, reading, listening, and so forth. Independent learning is a result of making informed opinions and finding pleasure in the arts. According to Rafoth (2001), "Teachers [and school library media specialists] can inspire independent learning through easy, often subtle, techniques that gently place responsibility for learning in the hands of students and teach them how to help themselves learn" (p. 15). When students succeed, their motivation and confidence rises and they learn to enjoy taking control of their learning. Rafoth (2001) also makes this statement regarding independent learning: "Teachers [and school library media specialists] play an important role in enabling their students to develop independent learning strategies, often by imparting simple strategies that can easily be embedded into the classroom routine. They must be aware of what students can and should achieve at different metacognitive stages in their lives. The strategies that students learn in the upper grades are inherently more complex than what they can master in the early grades. However, these more complex strategies are based on the recitation and other simple strategies they have learned as younger students. Finally, teachers [and school library media specialists] must take particular care not to discourage the kinds of questions and activities that help students become independent learners" (p. 21). We must inspire independent learning in our students so they can continue the process of lifelong learning. The following sources are valuable in helping you acquire more (and varied) information about independent learning and information literacy:

PRINT

Barron, D. D. (2001). *Thanks for the connections: Now are we information literate?* School Library Media Activities Monthly, 18(3), 49–51. *This article discusses the role of libraries in promoting information access and information literacy. It also includes useful Web sites that assist librarians in implementing "Information Power" and the information literacy standards.*

Callison, D. (2001). *Integrated instruction.* School Library Media Activities Monthly, 17(5), 33–39. *This article includes a history of course-related integrated instruction, isolated instruction, individual instruction, collaborative planning with other teachers, and independent inquiry that can lead to lifelong learning.*

Jones, C. (2001). *Infusing information literacy and technology into your school library media program.* Knowledge Quest, 30(1), 32–33. *This article focuses on infusing technology and instructional strategies into a school library media program. It is aimed at K–5 students and discusses a tool that fosters a pre-reader's independent access to resources and other useful tips.*

Kresberg, S. (2001). *Faculty-library media specialist cooperation or collaboration.* School Library Media Activities Monthly, 18(1), 22–25. *This article considers the differences in meaning between* collaboration *and* cooperation *and suggests methods to help library media specialists collaborate with faculty members.*

Latrobe, K., & Masters, A. (2001). *A case study of one district's implementation of Information Power.* School Library Media Research, 4. *This case study documents the initial implementation of "Information Power."*

Lehman, K., & Dudley, J. (2001). *Collaborating for information literacy.* Knowledge Quest, 30(1), 24–25. *This article describes a Web-based database project that houses lessons created by more than 30 elementary school library media specialists. It includes two sections: Literature Appreciation and Information Skills.*

Line, M. B. (2000). *The lifelong learner and the future library.* New Review of Libraries and Lifelong Learning, 1, 56–80. *This article identifies information literacy as a critical skill for independent learning. It outlines characteristics of the ideal library for lifelong learners for resources, access, and services.*

Martin, J. (2001). Information literacy news flash. School Library Media Activities Monthly, *17(5), 22. This article focuses on the use of the television show* The Barton Chapel Morning News Show *to provide students a means for applying information literacy, independent learning, and social responsibility standards.*

NON-PRINT

United States Department of Education. (2002). No child left behind *[Online]. Available: http://www.nochildleftbehind.gov. On January 8, 2002, President Bush changed the federal government's role in P–12 education by asking America's schools to describe their success by what each student accomplishes.*

United States Department of Education. (2001). Put reading first *[Online]. Available: http://www.nifl.gov/partnershipforreading/ publications/reading_first1.html. This site applies to K–3 children and summarizes what researchers discovered about how to teach children to read successfully. This research provides building blocks for teaching children to read.*

SCENARIOS

Let's look at practical, down-to earth ways and methods that school library media specialists can use to assist students with *independent,* socially responsible learning.

Information Power's Standard 4 explains that the student who is an independent learner applies the principles of information literacy to access, evaluate, and use information about issues and situations of personal interest (ALA, 1998). The following are three scenarios—one for a high school, one for a middle school, and one for an elementary school situation that relate to this standard.

High School: *Joe, a junior high school student, comes into the school library media center after his last class and requests assistance from the school librarian, Mr. Saul.*

Mr. Saul: Hi Joe, it is good to see you this afternoon. How can I help you?

Joe: Hi, Mr. Saul. I have been thinking about where I might want to go to college next year. I kind of know what I want to be, but I don't know the best schools for it. Where do I look?

Mr. Saul: First, what do you want to be?

Joe: I want to go into law…but something like international law.

Mr. Saul: Great! That sounds like an interesting and exciting career.

Joe: Yes, I'd really like to go into that field. I heard that there are some books and Internet sites that tell about colleges and universities and what they offer.

Mr. Saul: You're right. Here is what I am going to do for you. I have three CD-ROMs that should help, called *Peterson's College Database, Lovejoy's College Counselor,* and *The College Handbook.* I will get you started with these CD-ROMs. You can explore them and take notes. If you want to investigate it more thoroughly, I have written down several Web sites that also contain information about colleges and universities (www.collegenet.com, www.allaboutcollege.com, and www.theadmissionsoffice.com). Do you feel comfortable using the CD-ROMs and Internet?

Joe: Sure, that's perfect, Mr. Saul! I will begin today, but I may need to come back a few more days to look more thoroughly.

Mr. Saul: That's fine. Good luck. If you run into any problems, I will be available.

Joe: Thank you very much. This is great, Mr. Saul!

Teachers, the LMC, and Skill Development

The library media center can enrich the learning experience for students and make them more confident, independent learners—but only if they have the skills to use it successfully.

Most students do not automatically pick up the full range of information skills they need. However, these skills can be developed if teachers set out to:

> *Decide on key skills to be developed when drawing up schemes of work and planning projects and assignments. The skills chosen will influence the resources required and the activities selected.*

Provide opportunities for students to practice these skills in an appropriate subject context.

Devote discussion time to exploring how students apply the skills and particularly how they can build on their existing strategies. Teachers tend to be good at providing practice opportunities, but not so good at reflecting with students on the skills use.

Build feedback on student skills development into assessment.

Research has shown that although students necessarily employ a range of information skills in doing any project, they can only focus on a few. Choices have to be made about which skills should be developed at any given time. Relatively short practice and reflection activities can be introduced into lessons or projects to develop students' information skills.

Sneaky Teaching: The Librarian's Role
Act as a role model of good information searching

Reject the temptation to find it for them because it's quicker

Give support and encouragement

Give advice

Help students to evaluate the relevance of the information they have found through questions about relevance to task

Be aware of the marks scheme for units of work and point out that copying will not meet the criteria set

Remind students to make a note of their sources

(For more information, go to http://www.etln.org.uk/page23.html)

Middle School: *Sarah, a seventh-grade student, comes to the school library media center one morning before first period to talk to the school library media specialist, Mrs. Ben, about an upcoming vacation she and her family would like to take this summer.*

Mrs. Ben: Good morning, Sarah, how are you this morning?

Sarah: Fine, thank you. I want to ask you how to find something.

Mrs. Ben: Great. What is it you need to find?

Sarah: My family and I are going on a vacation this summer. We don't know where. All we know is somewhere in the United States. I have heard that there are some books and Web sites that can help me. I told my family I would do the research this year.

Mrs. Ben: That's terrific! Here is what we will do. I have some books to show you. Most of them are about specific places, but I will also write down quite a few Web sites that will give you a broader search. (The books: *Fodor's New York City, Fodor's Road Guides USA: Great American Drives of the West, Frommer's USA, Dorling Kindersley's Guias Visuales: San Francisco,* and *Sehlinger's The Unofficial Guide to Walt Disney World*). (The Web sites are www.mapsonus.com, www.mapquest.com, and http://maps.expedia.com/OverView.asp.) Do you feel comfortable with this?

Sarah: Oh, sure. This is exactly what I want! I just needed someone to get me started and point me in the right direction. I know lots about the Internet, so that will not be a problem.

Mrs. Ben: Wonderful. Take your time and remember that I am available if you run into any problems.

Elementary School: *Tori, a third-grade student, visits the school library media center one afternoon and asks the school library media specialist, Mr. Ross, if he can help her find some information about horses. This is not for a report. Tori stated that she just wants to learn more about them because someday she would like to own and ride some of her own.*

Mr. Ross: Hi Tori. How are you this afternoon?

Tori: Fine, Mr. Ross. Can you help me find something?

Mr. Ross: I will sure try. What are you looking for?

Tori: I want to find out some information about horses because when I grow up, I want to own and ride them. It doesn't have to be a lot right now. I just want some general information about horses first.

Mr. Ross: Ok. That will be no problem. Here is what I will do. I will guide you to a few encyclopedias (print ones): *Childcraft, Grolier's The New Book of Knowledge,* and *Oxford Chil-*

dren's Encyclopedia. Tori, I also have an encyclopedia on CD-ROM and I will get you started on that: *World Book Multimedia Encyclopedia.* Oh, I also know of some books about horses in the library: *Girls and Their Horses: True Stories from American Girl, DK Pockets: Horses,* and *Album of Horses.* Do you think that will be enough for a beginning?

Tori: Oh, yes, Mr. Ross. This is wonderful. May I check out the three books?

Mr. Ross: Certainly. If you have any questions, I will be here until 4:30 P.M.

What occurred in these three scenarios? The school library media specialist assisted the students, but they also *promoted independent learning.* Any of these school library media specialists could have looked up the information and handed it to the student. However, that would not have helped the students learn to be independent learners, and it would not have helped you (in the long run), as these students are becoming independent learners and will not rely on your assistance (as much!) in the future.

Standard 5 in *Information Power* states the following: "The student who is an independent learner applies the principles of information literacy to access, evaluate, enjoy, value and create artistic products" (ALA, 1998, p. 26). Let's look at another scenario to demonstrate how a school library media specialist can accomplish this.

Barbie Styers, a second-grade teacher, would like to make her Native American unit more applicable to each student. In the past, they discussed Native Americans and the students wrote a short report about one aspect of Native Americans. Mrs. Styers approaches the school library media specialist, Amy Real, with this situation.

Amy Real: Hi Barbie. What can I do for you today?

Barbie Styers: Amy, I have been teaching the Native American's unit for seven years now. I am tired of doing it the same old way—and I can tell my students are, too. I certainly know the content, but could use some assistance with fresh techniques. Can you help me figure out something different and more fun to do with this unit of study? Of course, as you know, state standards mandate specific learning by students, but I believe it can still be exciting and original.

Amy Real: Certainly. Let's work on this together. I will gather viable resources and you can assist me by providing state standards—keeping me on track —so to speak. As a team, we can make this a unique opportunity for your students!

Barbie Styers: Great. Let's work together Thursday afternoon, ok?

Amy Real: Sure!

Amy Real: (Thursday) Hi Barbie. I think I have some great resources for your Native American unit.

Barbie Styers: Fantastic! I am anxious to hear them—and I am ready with the state standards.

Amy Real: It seems that this unit could use a wider variety of resources—I know in the past, students just used encyclopedias and a few books. I have located a video about Cherokee Indians, a CD-ROM regarding Native Americans that is very interactive and fun, and a large number of Web sites regarding all sorts of issues surrounding Native Americans. I was also able to borrow a great set of books about Native Americans from another school library media center. In addition, I was thinking that we could change how the students are assessed. Instead of reports, why not give them choices about how they express what they know? For example, some students might dress up and create a short play, some may perhaps draw, paint, or sculpt, some issue concerning Native Americans, some may even write a short story of their own (fiction or nonfiction) about them. I also know that you have a few students who know technology well. Perhaps they could create a PowerPoint presentation. These are merely a few examples—the list could go on and on. In the end, we will have a wide variety of formats, the students will enjoy learning, they will be able to express themselves in whatever creative manner they wish, and they will become more independent learners. What do you think?

Barbie Styers: This is terrific! It fits perfectly into the state standards and our curricular goals. I can think of three of my students already who would love to create a PowerPoint presentation—and one who would love to create a play—and, oh,

I have one student who is an excellent artist. I am already excited! I know my students will have a good time producing a project of their own—it gives them freedom and a chance to be creative. I will begin the lesson plan today and share it with you Monday. Thank you so much, Amy.

Amy Real: You're welcome. Let me know what I can do to help...and don't forget to invite me to their presentations!

In this scenario, students are learning a topic by viewing a variety of formats and are allowed to present their understanding of Native Americans creatively, capitalizing on each student's and format's particular strength. The students are working *independently*.

Another portion of Standard 5 involves reading for pleasure. As a school library media specialist, you should promote recreational reading. Even more important, you should promote recreational reading in the content areas and provide access to popular resources. Students are often reluctant to ask for help in locating a leisure reading book. As a school library media specialist, use a positive approach and generously offer your help to students. In addition, learn to use all the tools for promoting books and reading available to you. You should also create an environment in the school library media center that encourages students to read and helps them find the right book. Six examples of helpful resources for teachers and school library media specialists are the following:

Bromann, J. (2001). Booktalking that works. *New York: Neal-Schuman.*

Knowles, E., & Smith, M. (2001). Reading rules!: Motivating teens to read. *Englewood, CO: Libraries Unlimited.*

Miller, P. (2001). Reaching every reader: Promotional strategies for the elementary school library media specialist. *Worthington, OH: Linworth.*

Schell, L. (2001). Booktalks plus: Motivating teens to read. *Englewood, CO: Libraries Unlimited.*

Volz, B. D., Scheer, C. P., & Welborn, L. B. (2000). Junior Genreflecting: A guide to good reads and series fiction for children. *Englewood, CO: Libraries Unlimited.*

Weissman, A. (2002). Do tell! Storytelling for you and your students. *Worthington, OH: Linworth.*

A few rather effortless ways to promote recreational reading are the following:

> Collect book lists. Photocopy them and put them in a binder as a display for student use.
>
> Create a "If you liked..." list. For example, you might put, "If you liked the book *The Giver* by Lois Lowry, you might like to look at some books written by Madeline L'Engle." This will help students branch out in their choices of leisure reading.
>
> Have students create a list of book reviews (peer or professional). Post the list around the school library media center.
>
> Put up posters about reading or certain books. Surround the poster with books that are similar.
>
> Display bestsellers or various genres. Make the display(s) appealing and exciting to young people.

I am sure that you can create other ways to promote creative expressions of information—use your imagination!

Information Power's Standard 6 states, "The student who is an independent learner applies the principles of information literacy to evaluate and use his or her own information processes and products as well as those developed by others. That student actively and independently reflects on and critiques personal thought processes and individually created information products" (ALA, 1998, p. 29). The following scenario may further explain this statement:

Carol and Phil, both junior high school students, have been coming to the school library media center during their English class period for the past week. They are working on a report together about major natural disasters in the United States during the past 50 years. One day, they approach the school library media specialist, Ms. Cole, explaining that something is not right about their report.

Carol and Phil: Ms. Cole, as you know, we have been working on a project all week, but we now both agree that something is wrong. Can you help us?

Ms. Cole: Sure, I will be happy to. Explain what you think is wrong. What is the problem?

Carol and Phil: Well, we are writing about major natural disasters in the United States over the past 50 years. It is very interesting and we have found lots and lots of information about these disasters. But now we are trying to write the report, and it just seems so dull. I mean these disasters were incredible—we saw a video about one earthquake and a laserdisc about a volcano and lots of cool pictures on the Internet about other natural disasters. It's really hard to describe them in words.

Ms. Cole: Did your English teacher say that you must turn in a written report?

Carol and Phil: Well, no, not really. I guess we just thought that is what we should do. What else could we do?

Ms. Cole: First, let's get permission from your teacher and we will talk about it tomorrow, ok?

Carol and Phil: That sounds great. See you tomorrow.

Ms. Cole: (next day) As you probably know, your teacher welcomes the idea of an alternative to a written report.

Carol and Phil: Yeah, we know—that's super. What suggestions do you have for us?

Ms. Cole: Well, you said that words are "not doing the job." What might depict major natural disasters in the United States more effectively?

Carol: Oh, I know, we need to show them visuals. How could we do that?

Phil: I've got an idea! You taught us how to create a Power-Point last year—remember?—and I've learned how to add video, pictures, everything!

Carol: That's great, Phil. I can help you organize it—we learned all about graphic organizers earlier this year, right?

Ms. Cole: I think you've got the perfect idea! Major natural disasters gain more interest and have more meaning and authenticity when you have visuals accompanying the words. Don't forget to invite me to your presentation!

Carol: Thanks a million, Ms. Cole. Let's get started, Phil!

Carol and Phil reflected on their work and revised it based on feed-back. They modified their presentation to make it more authentic, meaningful, and exciting. Carol and Phil thought of strategies to improve their work. They, too, are becoming *independent learners.*

Independent learning can begin at a very young age. School library media specialists (and teachers) provide guidance and students assume the responsibility for their own study and learning. Yes, this is yet another role change. You, as a school library media specialist, must assist students in learning for themselves.

5

In Life

INTRODUCTION

Standards 7, 8, and 9 as stated in *Information Power: Building Partnerships for Learning*, are as follows:

> *The student who contributes positively to the learning community and to society is information literate and recognizes the importance of information to a democratic society.*
>
> *The student who contributes positively to the learning community and to society is information literate and practices ethical behavior in regard to information and information technology.*
>
> *The student who contributes positively to the learning community and to society is information literate and participates effectively in groups to pursue and generate information. (AASL & AECT, 1998, pp. 38–39)*

What is democracy? What is social responsibility? How does it differ from any other responsibility? How does social responsibility relate to information literacy? These are viable and often-overlooked questions. First, what actually is democracy? One definition is that democracy is a creative and constructive process for which students need practical judgment, a shared fund of civic knowledge, and deliberative skills and dispositions—much of which must be learned in schools. Next, social responsibility pertains to ethics and morals of all students—citizens. The ALA (1998) speaks of social responsibility aligned with democracy, ethical behavior, and contributing to society. Social responsibility differs from other responsibilities in that it involves—deeply involves— the lives of others. What does social responsibility have to do with information literacy—LOTS! In our society today, students are allowed the opportunity to retrieve enormous amounts of information with the click of a key. This was not true 30 years ago. Therefore, students can take advantage of this by plagiarizing—or they can become responsible citizens who behave ethically and contribute (not take away from) our current information flow. As explained in *Information Power,* not only does an information literate student "understand that access to information is basic to the functioning of a democracy" (ALA, 1998, p. 33), but a student "applies principles and practices that reflect high ethical standards for accessing, evaluating, and using information" (p. 36) and "shares information and ideas across a range of sources and perspectives and acknowledges the insights and contributions of a variety of cultures and disciplines" (p. 39).

Tanner wrote an article entitled "Standards, Standards: High and Low" in 1997. Although this article primarily addresses standardization woes, one statement asks a fundamental question: "What knowledge is of most worth? Strange it is indeed that contemporary education reformers are beginning at the end by formulating standards to be attained without asking the curriculum question of questions: 'What knowledge is of most worth?'—to which might be added, 'for the development of enlightened, productive, and responsible citizens in a free society?' This in turn would require the development of the many emergent pathways and means (curriculum) to develop the outcomes" (p. 118). Tanner continues by explaining, "Then there remains the nagging question: Even if the child should be capable of meeting certain standards of 'content knowledge' such as 'the impact of trade networks on Mesopotamia,' should the child be required to study for this end, or should the child be learning something that relates integrally with his or her life and growth and life in society? ... Schools must be dedicated to the release of students' fullest possible potentials for growth in personal and social insight for democratic social responsibility" (p. 118).

Social responsibility is also entwined with critical thinking and problem-solving. Langford (2001) points this out explicitly: "However we view critical literacy, it must center on thought and our belief that, through developing the processes of thinking, our attitudes will be shaped. Our values and beliefs, coupled with the ability to solve problems, are partners in developing and shaping our worldview. And this sharpening and developing of our worldview critically asks us to appraise our information environment...Let us acknowledge a paradigm shift from information skills thinking to lifelong learning thinking, complete with the metacognitive skills of critical literacy: critical and creative thinking. Let us truly set our young people onward towards the goal of functioning well in society...this is a far more regenerative concept for educators to be a part of than some narrowly defined information literacy concept" (pp. 20–21).

SOCIAL RESPONSIBILITY

What does ethical mean? According the *Merriam-Webster Dictionary,* ethical means conforming to accepted professional standards or modes of conduct. Teaching students to behave ethically and morally is not a new phenomenon. What is new is that in our information-overloaded society, where anyone can write anything with the right tools and equipment, and information is so readily accessible, behaving ethically is more challenging for students. *Plagiarism* is easier to accomplish in today's technological world. What is plagiarism? It is simply turning in someone else's work as your own. *It is dishonest and illegal.* Remember, however that this does not mean that students cannot use a portion of someone else's work. It is perfectly acceptable to borrow someone else's idea IF the student gives him or her proper credit. Plagiarism is using without permission. Students need to learn how to paraphrase, summarize, use quotes appropriately, and cite where information originated. This should be a shared effort between the school librarian and teacher. However, as a school library media specialist, you may need to take the first step. Numerous Web sites can assist you in this endeavor (see later).

With the advent of the Internet, "paper mills" have followed. What is a paper mill? "Internet paper mill Web sites provide papers at no cost or for a fee. You should be aware, however, that instructors [and school library media specialists] are now better equipped to detect use of these sites" (Riedling, 2002, p. 89). Web sites now exist that catch plagiarism, such as Turnitin.com (http://www.turnitin.com).

As Minkel (2002) wrote, "A May 2001 Rutgers University survey of 4,471 high school students discovered that more than half had stolen sentences and paragraphs from the Internet and 74 percent admitted to cheating on a test. While there's no denying that the Web has emerged as the resource of choice for most students, librarians and teachers must take it upon themselves to avoid plagiarism before the epidemic spreads" (p. 50). School library media specialists must explain plagiarism to students and tell them why it is unethical and dishonest. It may perhaps be helpful to make it practical—even personal. For example, have students create a story or picture or play and place it on the World Wide Web. Then ask the students how they would feel if that story, picture, or play were found on another Web site with someone else's name. What would they think? Does it feel more unethical and dishonest? Students must also learn useful research skills—by teachers or school library media specialists. They must be taught how to conduct research effectively and efficiently (become information literate!). In addition, teachers (and school library media specialists) need to give students assignments that require the use of a variety of sources and formats—and at the same time require critical thinking, and problem-solving skills. Students need to learn to interpret, analyze, and synthesize information. It is your job, as a school library media specialist (again, *one* of your jobs!), to make this happen. The following sources can be useful regarding plagiarism, proper citations, and effective study skills:

PRINT

Callison, D. (1999). *Reflection.* School Library Media Activities Monthly, 16(2), 30–33. *This article discusses reflection as the key both to the student process for learning effective use of information and for the teacher/school library media specialist who wants to evaluate his or her techniques for instruction in information literacy.*

Groark, M., Oblinger, D., & Choa, M. (2001). *Term paper mills, anti-plagiarism tools, and academic integrity.* Educause Review,

36(5), 40–48. This article focuses on the issue of cheating, plagiarism, and academic integrity in the United States.

Janowski, A. (2002, September). Plagiarism: Prevention, not prosecution. Book Report 21(2), 26. This article discusses how to deal proactively with the issue of plagiarism.

Lincoln, M. (2002). Internet plagiarism: An agenda for staff in-service and student awareness. MultiMedia Schools, 9(1), 46–49. This article discusses Internet plagiarism and includes an outline for a presentation that library media specialists can use with teachers.

Riedling, A. M. (2003). Helping teachers teach students about ethical behavior. Teacher Librarian, 30(5), 42–44.

NONPRINT

The Center for Academic Integrity [Online]. Available: http://www.academicintegrity.org/cai_research.asp. Research projects conducted by Donald L. McCabe of Rutgers University (founder and first president of CAI), have had disturbing, provocative, and challenging results. This Web site discusses these projects.

Example of an Internet Paper Mill, offering custom-made papers for a fee [Online]. Available: http://www.academictermpapers. com. "Academic Term Papers offers the Web's largest selection of research papers (over 30,000 on file at the lowest rates): Only $7.00 per page."

Example of an Internet Paper Mill, offering free term papers, essays, and reports [Online]. Available: http://www.cyberessays.com. "Cyber Essays is your one-stop source for free, high-quality term papers, essays, and reports on all subjects. Please use either the available paper categories or our database search to find the paper you need quickly and easily."

The Instructors Guide to Internet Plagiarism [Online]. Available: http://www.plagiarized.com. The purpose of this site is to help teachers or professors (or even parents) determine if a given piece of academic work has been obtained from the Internet.

> *Johnson, D. (2004, January). Proactively teaching technology ethics. Library Media Connection [Online]. Available: http://www. linworth.com/lmc.html. This article provides a proactive approach to ethical issues for students.*
> Plagiarism Stoppers: A Teachers Guide *[Online]. Available: http://www.ncusd203.org/central/html/where/plagiarism_stoppers. html. This Web site offers places to go for help with student plagiarism, how to identify it, what to do when it happens, and how to prevent it.*
> Using Sources for a Research paper *[Online]. Available: http://www.hamilton.edu/academic/Resource/WC/UsingOutside Sources.html. This site begins, "It is essential… that every student understand the standards of academic honesty and how to avoid dishonesty by proper acknowledgment of intellectual indebtedness."*
> Virtual Salt: Anti-Plagiarism Strategies for Research Papers *[Online]. Available: http://www.virtualsalt.com/antiplag.htm. The strategies discussed in this site can be used to combat what some believe is an increasing amount of plagiarism on research papers. By employing these strategies, one can help encourage stu dents to value the assignment and to do their own work.*

RESEARCH AND DEVELOPMENT

McGregor and Streitenberger (1998) conducted two studies that focused on plagiarism in high schools. One study took place in a high school in Alberta, Canada, in 1993; the second study took place in a Texas high school in 1996. Overall, the studies compared students' final papers with the original sources of information. The Texas study examined particular findings of the Canada study. One group received little direction in proper citation and the avoidance of plagiarism. The other group was very conscious of the need to cite properly and to avoid plagiarism because of emphasis by the teacher. The result: Students in group one tended to copy directly from original sources. In the original (Canada) study, an apparent connection between a process/product orientation of a particular student and the way in which that student used information was investigated further in the second (Texas) study. All students in the [first] study demonstrated an orientation toward the format of the product rather than the process of gathering and synthesizing information for the content. Students were concerned about making their product fit the mold they envisioned based on prior experience and the instructions for the assignment. Those students who demonstrated little or no awareness of the processes, such as seeking meaning, making sense, or learning, tended to exhibit a strong desire to make the final product look good or sound right. These same students tended to copy a great deal from the original sources of information rather than paraphrase the information or synthesize the ideas. On the other hand, the students who demonstrated involvement in processes of seeking meaning, making sense, or learning did not copy from their sources. They synthesized, summarized, and paraphrased the information.

What do these studies tell us? Plagiarism is avoidable with proper instruction regarding summarizing, paraphrasing, and seeking meaning from information. As school library media specialists, we must be *leaders* concerning these issues. We must assist teachers and students to ultimately be *socially responsible* citizens. How is this accomplished? There is no one answer. It is useful to provide information to students concerning plagiarism and copyright—paraphrasing and summarizing, and it is necessary to teach them these important skills.

The following are articles that pertain to social responsibility and information literacy:

Barron, D. D. (1998). So what does the research say about school library media concerns? School Library Media Activities Monthly, 14(5), 47–50. *This article includes an annotated bibliography of research related to school library media programs, such as intellectual freedom, social responsibilities, information literacy, and so forth.*

Barron, D. D. (2002). The library media specialist, Information Power, and social responsibility: Part 1(plagiarism). School Library Media Activities Monthly, 18(6), 48. *This article discusses the concepts surrounding helping children to become information literate and independent learners for life. It also emphasizes students being active, positive contributors to our democratic way of life.*

Clyde, A. (2001). *Electronic plagiarism.* Teacher Librarian, 29(1), 32–33. *This article presents a list of Web sites that provide information about electronic plagiarism and what can be done about it.*

Fialkoff, F., & St. Evan, L. (2002). *Bringing order to an unruly web.* Library Journal, 127(7), 2–5. *This article discusses widespread instances of student plagiarism, the role of the Internet in plagiarism, and the importance of library media centers (and library media specialists) in preventing the misuse of information.*

Gardiner, S. (2001). *Cybercheating: A new twist on an old problem.* Phi Delta Kappan, 83(2), 172–174. *This article offers advice on detecting when students have plagiarized research papers from the Internet.*

Children can learn to be socially responsible at a very young age. This may involve (for a five-year-old, for example) saying, "I'm sorry" for hurting someone or breaking another student's toy. Teaching social responsibility (in general) can be taught using numerous exercises and tactics. According to Yeager and Silva (2002), the following activities (summarized) can help elementary-age students achieve a broader understanding of democracy and social responsibility:

Have children sit together in a circle and learn how to talk with each other in respectful ways about their concerns and any problems that may have arisen in the classroom. Talk about the problem(s) and attempt to find a solution(s).

Organize panel discussions of different perspectives on a specific issue.

Pose questions such as "What is fairness?," "What is justice?," "What are some things that happen that are unjust?," and "Why do you think these things are unjust?"

Take a field trip to the local courthouse to visit the judge's chamber. Children learn about decision-making processes and how the jury system works.

Help students distinguish between types of unfairness and injustice (things that affect oneself, thinks that affect a lot of people, things that seem easy to work on, things that seem difficult to solve).

Have students visit the following Web site: www.unicef.org/voy, Voices of Youth, which helps develop awareness about issues and crises confronting children around the world and interacts with children from other countries.

Use young adult literature to visit the lives of other people who have struggled with issues of fairness and justice.

Develop classroom service clubs. Working in cooperative groups, students can develop the club's focus and constitution to focus on the elements central to a strong democracy.

Have the students coordinate and implement a book drive for a local homeless shelter.

Take a group of students to perform reader's theatre at a nearby senior citizen's center.

Even young students are capable of understanding the complexity of social responsibility. Children can gain a sense that democracy needs citizens with deliberative skills, concerns about fairness and justice, and a sense of social responsibility by participating in age-appropriate activities that "challenge them to care about others, about ideas, and about the world around them" (Yeager & Silva, 2002).

What do you *do* to help students become socially responsible, ethical, and honest? Providing information (teaching students about ethical behavior) is always a good beginning—prevention is easier than dealing with the situation. Beach (2001) provides some ideas about how to help students:

Search the Internet to find out the types of materials available on the topic you've assigned.

Structure the assignment so it lends itself less to direct copying.

Collect an in-class student writing sample at the beginning of the year.

Discuss and teach about plagiarism [in your school library media center].

Review and distribute the school's policy on plagiarism, including consequences.

Make completion of an online tutorial on plagiarism a classroom assignment.

Practice paraphrasing [and summarizing].

Require students to use a print resource first.

Require students to turn in bibliography cards, note cards, photocopies of sources, and outlines with the final paper. (pp. 1–2)

Let's look at a possible scenario between a principal and a school library media specialist.

The principal, Ms. Lorie Reyes, approaches the school librarian, Mr. Rich Leigh, regarding plagiarism in their urban middle school. Ms. Reyes believes that it has become a "real problem" and wants Mr. Leigh to assist in whatever ways he can to combat this serious issue.

Lorie: Hi Rich. How are things in the media center? I see lots of activity when I pass by!

Rich: Going very well, thank you. Yes, we have a busy library—and that's just the way I like it!

Lorie: I have a concern I want to discuss with you. I believe that plagiarism has become a severe problem at our school. I know it is not totally your responsibility, but I wondered if you could come up with some ways to combat it. Any ideas?

Rich: Sure. Off the top of my head, I believe teachers would benefit from a workshop—or some type of instruction—regarding such issues as summarizing, paraphrasing, citing sources, website evaluation, paper mills, proper questioning techniques and so forth.

Lorie: That sounds great! I know of two teachers who would be happy to work with you on this project. This is an excellent idea—beginning with the teachers to get the ball rolling. I will be happy to help you any way I can. Can you put something in writing—even an outline—in the next couple of weeks?

Rich: Absolutely! I will work on it. I am glad to have the teacher support. We certainly need "buy in" from teachers, staff, and administrators to create socially responsible students.

Lorie: I certainly agree. I will keep in close contact and begin spreading the word.

Teaching social responsibility cannot occur in a vacuum. Rich (and Lorie) are correct about building a community of believers to create ethical students. Many times, teachers (and students) are unaware of how to combat plagiarism. It is everyone's duty to work on social responsibility, but the school librarian often must take the lead. Our global, technological world has made plagiarism easier than ever before. Education, not only of students—but school staff—is critical to success.

Among the many, many things we teach as school library media specialists, social responsibility ranks near the top (if not number *one*). We are responsible for teaching information and about information, but we are also the *leaders,* the *role models* for many of these teachers and students. Therefore, it is critical that we act socially responsible and teach our teachers and students the same. Our world has certainly changed over time, but the rules remain identical.

To assist with promoting socially responsible teachers and students, the following are more helpful tips:

Become aware of what social responsibility entails.

Recognize that procrastination is a large part of plagiarism (social responsibility).

Effective research strategies and writing skills help people to become socially responsible.

Use a variety of resources to prevent plagiarism.

Questioning skills (by teachers) are critical with regard to producing socially responsible students.

Taking notes and producing drafts before actual research is completed diminishes plagiarism.

Learn to cite sources—even if you are unsure if they should be cited!

Teach students to not succumb to pressures from peers or others.

Make students feel proud of their work.

Always be available to help students with questions/concerns about social responsibility.

6

In Motion

INTRODUCTION

According to Anderson (1999), "Media programs are no longer measured by the number of books in the school library media center, but by the information literacy level of the students. Student learning is achieved through the collaborative and proactive leadership roles of the school library media specialist, not merely by cataloging and organizing materials. The most tangible portion of *Information Power: Building Partnerships for Learning* is the cogent description given of the information literate student presented as a series of nine articulate standards, each with its own indicators and proficiency levels" (p. 22). This is precisely what this book is all about—school library media specialists and information literacy, namely the student who is

Information literate: Accesses information efficiently and effectively

Information literate: Evaluates information critically and competently

Information literate: Uses information accurately and creatively

An independent learner: Pursues information related to personal interests

An independent learner: Appreciates literature and other creative expressions of information

An independent learner: Strives for excellence in information seeking and knowledge generation

Socially responsible: Contributes positively to the learning community and to society; recognizing the importance of information to a democratic society

Socially responsible: Practices ethical behavior regarding information and information technology

Socially responsible: Participates effectively in groups to pursue and generate information

THINKING AHEAD

The following are some interesting statistics by Cattagni and Farris (2001) on behalf of the National Center for Educational Statistics, from *Internet Access in U.S. Public Schools and Classrooms: 1994–2000.*

By the fall of 2000, 98% of public schools were connected to the Internet (compared to 35% in 1994).

By the fall of 2000, the ratio of students to instructional computers in public schools decreased to five to one. The ratio of students to instructional computers with Internet access in public schools improved from 9 to 1 in 1999 to 7 to 1 in 2000.

By 2000, 77% of the nation's public schools that were connected to the Internet used dedicated lines compared to 1996 when 74% of public schools used dial-up connections.

Secondary schools (86%) were more likely to use dedicated lines than elementary schools (74%),

In 2000, 54% of public schools with access to the Internet reported that computers with access to the Internet were available to students outside of regular school hours. Secondary schools were more likely to make the Internet available to students outside of regular school hours than elementary schools (80% compared to 46%).

Of all public schools with Internet access, 98% had "Acceptable Use Policies" and used technologies or procedures, such as blocking or filtering software, to control student access to inappropriate material on the Internet (p. 49)

These statistics are interesting and important. They are significant to know, BUT, being connected does not mean that students know how to use the connectivity. Information literacy *is not an innate knowledge. It must be developed.* School library media specialists play an *important* role in this development.

Why do we still need school library media specialists? Kranich remarks, "[They] are more popular than ever. Pollsters estimate that as many as 81% of Americans use [school library media centers] every year.... Perhaps a better question to ask is why the nation's 115,000 public, school, academic and special libraries are gaining in popularity.... [School library media centers] are the only place where information is freely available for everyone... [and] [they] provide personalized help and training.... More than ever our communities need [school library media specialists] to teach the information literacy skills vital for success in the 21st century.... [School library media specialists] are helping to build information-smart communities so that all Americans can thrive in the digital age. [School library media centers and school library media specialists] are vital to our economic well-being, to global understanding, to the advancement of learning, to meeting the challenge of information overload, to public participation in the democratic process, and to closing the digital divide" (2001, p. 7). Wow! How much more needs to be said? We, as school library media specialists, are not only important in the 21st century, we are *important!* Barron (2001) explained it this way: "The question becomes, Now that we have access, what do we [school library media specialists] do with it? And the answer is,... the [school library media specialist's] full employment act. As with every other medium created by humans, our job always has been to find the information our users want and get it to them in the most effective way possible.... The great thing that all this information suggests is that we have opportunities for communication and access to information that have no precedent. We have the potential to help our kids and teachers access almost anything that they may need to learn and to teach. Being connected, however, does not mean that they know how to use the connectivity. Information literacy is *not an innate* knowledge. It must be developed" (p. 50).

How did it begin? The school library media specialist profession's response to the proliferation of information was to reconfigure the library skills instruction programs of the 1960s into a research framework called information literacy (California Media and Library Educators Association, 1994). Kapitzke (2001) argues that information literacy should not be the domain of the school library media specialist alone and that training in it should be integrated across all subject areas. Kapitzke continues to explain that libraries are not only affected by technological change, but also by social and cultural change. Information literacy is not about diagnostic thinking or impartial cognitive processes, but about helping students to design and forge life words in a range of text-based communities and economies. School library media specialists need to shift their focal points from a concern for a single, dominant theory of information literacy to the social and cultural construction of its pedagogies.

The *School Library Journal* staff conducted a survey to decide the top issues for those who provide library service to children and young adults (Ishizuka, Minkel, & St. Lifer, 2002). These authors distilled five themes that represent the profession's overriding challenges for 2002. One of them is as follows: "Making information literacy a higher priority among teachers and an essential, required skill for students" (p. 51).

Pryor relates information literacy (*Information Power: Building Partnerships for Learning* [AASL & AECT, 1998]) to Peter Senge's *The Fifth Discipline*. Each of the five disciplines is examined relative to the leadership role of school library media specialists and school library media centers. Pryor (2001) states,

> Shared Vision or what do we want may be described as the school library media specialist's vision of information literacy as defined by *Information Power*. Information literacy, or the ability to find and use information for learning, is central to the school library media [center] program.
>
> Personal Mastery is a discipline that requires the school library media specialist to continually expand the shared vision through research, self-understanding, and personal development.

Mental Models requires the school library media specialist to reflect upon, clarify, and improve the actions and decisions that shape the information literacy vision.

Team Learning is the process of creating results through communication and collaboration. Resource-based planning provides the school library media specialist with the perfect opportunity to transform student achievement results through communication and collaboration.

Systems Thinking integrates the other disciplines into a complete practice by relating patterns that connect the school library media center to the larger process within the learning community.

The "learning organization" model presented by Peter Senge recognizes that schools are complex systems with many leaders. The school library media specialist is a leader in the position to shape student learning through a vision of information literacy. (pp. 20–22)

The following Web sites, articles, and books are beneficial to learn more about information literacy—from numerous aspects—and research that has been recently conducted in this area:

PRINT

Atkins, P. (2001). Information literacy and the arts. College & Research Library News, *62(11), 1086. This article advises librarians how to foster information literacy in the arts and other disciplines.*

Barron, D. D. (1998). Information Power: Building partnerships for learning—our new vision, our new blueprint for school library media programs. School Library Media Activities Monthly, *15(1), 48–50. This article discusses* Information Power *as a document to be celebrated as school library media specialists' vision for learning, a blueprint for our profession, to be used on a daily basis, and to be shared with every member of our learning community.*

Barron, D. D. (2002). School library media research: 2000–2002. School Library Media Activities Monthly, *18(10), 48–50. This article provides an overview of several research papers on school library media centers from 2000 to 2002.*

Berger, P. (2002). Not your parents' library. Technology and Learning, *22(10), 48–49. This article examines the effects of technology on traditional school libraries.*

Branch, J. L., & Oberg, D. (2001). The teacher-librarian in the 21st century. School Libraries in Canada, *21(2), 14–18. This article discusses the role of the school media specialist as instructional leader; that leadership leads to collaboration. It provides current research and theory on information literacy instruction.*

Callison, D. (2000). Knowledge management. School Library Media Activities Monthly, *16(7), 37–39. This article discusses knowledge management and how it relates to the capacity of school library media specialists to act in a wide variety of situations with other educators as well as with their community and profession.*

Callison, D. (2002). Information inquiry. School Library Media Activities Monthly, *18(10), 35. This article deals with a learning method called information inquiry, which relates to the basics of information literacy.*

Farmer, L. S. J. (2002). Getting an early start on using technology for research. Library Talk, *15(2), 24–26. This article provides ways of helping students use computer technology for research.*

Farmer, L. S. J. (2002). Harnessing the power in information power. Teacher Librarian, *29(3), 20–25. This article discusses how the school library media specialist identifies information literacy and library program needs.*

Haycock, K. (2002). Positive role models and leadership. Teacher Librarian, *29(5), 35–40. This article discusses the views of pre-service teachers on information literacy instruction.*

Kearns, J. (2002). Volunteering for information literacy. Library Talk, *15(2), 19. This article discusses an information literacy program for fourth-grade students.*

Lau, D. (2002). Got clout? School Library Journal, *May, 40–45. This article discusses a survey that shows the increasing influence of school library media specialists.*

Marcum, J. W. (2002). Rethinking information literacy. Library Quarterly, *72(1), 1. This article focuses on the need to clarify the objectives of information literacy in the United States.*

Minkel, W. (2002). *Selling information literacy.* School Library Journal, 48*(2)*, 37. *This article discusses how to make information literacy skills important to teachers and students, while teaching students something meaningful about the Internet.*

Oldford, R. (2002). *Why institutionalization has failed.* Teacher Librarian, 28*(3)*, 8–15. *This article discusses the importance of a movement toward resource-based learning and information literacy.*

Plecas, B., & Ray, D. (2002). *Introduction.* School Libraries in Canada, 21*(3)*, 2. *This article discusses the ethics of information use.*

Troutner, J. (2002). *Information literacy activities and skills.* Teacher Librarian, 29*(5)*, 29. *This article presents several Web sites that will help teachers integrate information literacy activities and skills into lesson plans.*

Tschamler, A. (2002). *Top secret: Collaborative efforts really do make a difference.* Library Talk, 15*(2)*, 14–16. *This article discusses collaboration with teachers to teach information skills to students and the benefits of collaborative efforts for student learning.*

NONPRINT

The National Forum on Information Literacy *[Online]. Available: http://www.infolit.org. "The National Forum on Information Literacy was created in 1990 as a response to the recommendations of the American Library Association's Presidential Committee on Information Literacy."*

Texas Information Literacy Tutorial *[Online]. Available: http://tilt.lib.utsystem.edu. This interactive library tutorial prepares individuals to explore and research in the online world.*

Information Literacy Community Partnerships Toolkit *[Online]. Available: http://library.austin.cc.tx.us/staff/lnavarro/communitypartnerships/toolkit.html. The overall goal of this Web site is to build information literacy community partnerships. These partnerships will bring together librarians from school, academic, public, and special libraries and community members/organizations to help prepare the public to use information efficiently and effectively.*

RESEARCH AND DEVELOPMENT

Pickard (1993) explains, "The role of the school library media specialist has progressed from that of librarian...to master teacher, instructional design partner, or teacher librarian.... [However], even though the instructional role of the school library media specialist has evolved to one of prominence in the literature, research studies indicate discrepancies between theory and practice. Studies have shown a ten-year lag between the introduction of the concept and its actualization in the profession" (p. 1). There exist steps the school library media specialist can follow to play an important and central role in curriculum planning and development, including being aware of the total instructional program of the school. Examples are as follows:

Visiting classes as often as possible
Knowing the current methods of teaching
Becoming involved in the actual planning of the curriculum
Conducting in-service for teachers
Knowing bibliographies in the textbooks and adding books cited
    in them to the media center collection
Participating as a member of the instructional team

A research study was conducted within middle school library media centers in Cobb County, Georgia, regarding teacher/media specialist cooperation and services. The results showed that 83 percent of the responding school library media specialists had worked in a team-teaching situation in which ideas and responsibilities were shared to plan, develop, and implement student instruction, but only 11 percent of responding teachers had participated in such a unit. The study was significant in that results helped in assessing the success and justification of the DeKalb County Department of Educational Media's direct emphasis of "helping teachers teach," the term used by Turner (1993) and chosen by the department to encompass the instructional role of the library media specialist. *Information Power* defines the school library media specialist as information specialist, teacher, and instructional partner—giving equal importance to each role (ALA, 1998). The roles of teacher and instructional partner go hand-in-hand. An instructional partner must have the knowledge, expertise, and experience of a teacher combined with knowledge of the total library media collection and other resources outside the center that relate to and enhance the curriculum. School library media specialists should bring their knowledge of research, teaching methodology, curriculum development, learning theory, and instructional development to the entire process of teaching. Thus, the school library media specialist must be a master teacher. The literature goes further in applying the terms *instructional leader* and *instructional innovator* to the library media specialist. We may not yet be there, but we certainly appear to be moving in the right direction. As of January 2003, 435 school library media specialists had become National Board Certified by engaging in a rigorous certification process. This demonstrated the value of school librarians as instructional leaders; library media specialists value National Board Certification as a validation of their work as teachers.

WHAT NOW?

Technology (the author predicts) is not going to slow down. It is here for us (school library media specialists) to deal with—to learn and enjoy. It will continue (at least for quite a while) to be a medium for everyone—with no guidelines or consequences (a non-evaluated resource). This is not necessarily bad news. Wow! Students (and we) have so much information at their (our) fingertips from all over the world. How lucky to live in this generation! However, along with the good— all of the information—is the not-so good—MISinformation. Our role now— and in the foreseeable future—is to teach information literacy skills to our students. This book has discussed a variety of issues that are involved with information literacy. We must realize that we cannot teach every single student (or teacher, administrator, parent, etc.) to be information literate single-handed, but we must be *leaders—and entice collaboration within the school community.* School library media specialists are more important that ever— yes, YOU are more important than ever! Our world has been blessed with an incredible amount of information, but no guidelines came along with all of this information regarding use, access, evaluation, appreciation, and so forth—the information just came. As school library media specialists, we are again challenged. Isn't it wonderful to be needed and be a pioneer? We must possess the skills to teach students (and the school community) to be lifelong, independent learners. Is it easy? Probably not. Is it worthwhile? YOU BET! You are the leaders of the future of people functioning in the twenty-first century. What a lucky, *important* profession we have chosen!

References

AASL (American Association of School Librarians) & AECT (Association for Educational Communications and Technology). (1998). *Information power: Building partnerships for learning.* Chicago: American Library Association.

ALA (American Library Association). (1989). *Presidential committee on information literacy. Final report.* Chicago: American Library Association.

Anderson, M. A. (1999). Information power: Because student achievement is the bottom line. *MultiMedia Schools, 6*(2), 22–23.

Barron, D. D. (2001). Thanks for the connections: Now are we information literate? *School Library Media Activities Monthly, 18*(3), 49–51.

Beach, A. L. (2001). *Catch me if you can: A teacher's guide to preventing and detecting Internet plagiarism.* Spalding University Library Intern Project, Louisville, KY.

Breivik, P. S., & Senn, J. A. (1994). *Information literacy: Educating children for the 21st century.* New York: Scholastic.

Buzzeo, T. (2002a). *Collaborating to Meet Standards: Teacher/Librarian Partnerships for K–6.* Worthington, OH: Linworth.

Buzzeo, T. (2002b). *Collaborating to Meet Standards: Teacher/Librarian Partnerships for 7–12.* Worthington, OH: Linworth.

California Media and Library Educators Association. (1994). *From library skills to information literacy: A handbook for the 21st century.* Castle Rock, OH: H. Willow Research and Publishers.

Callison, D. (2001). Strategy: Search and comprehension. *School Library Media Activities Monthly, 1*(8), 32–36.

Castro, G. M. (2002). From workbook to web: Building an information literacy oasis. *Computers in Libraries, 22*(1), 30–36.

Cattagni, A., & Farris, E. (2001). *Internet access in U.S. public schools and classrooms: 1994–2000.* Washington, DC: National Center for Educational Statistics.

Doyle, C. S. (1994). *Information literacy in an information society: A concept for the information age.* Syracuse, NY: ERIC Clearinghouse on Information and Technology.

Eisenberg, M., & Brown, M. K. (1992). Current themes regarding library and information skills instruction: Research supporting and research lacking. *School Library Media Quarterly, 20*(2).

Ellis, K. V., & Lenk, M. A. (2001). Library media specialists: The keystone to integrating information technology and information literacy. *Independent School, 60*(4), 12–26.

Entwistle, N. (1981). *Styles of learning and teaching: An integrative outline of educational psychology.* Chichester, England: Wiley.

Henri, J., & Bonanno, K. (Eds.). (1999). *The information literate school community: Best practice.* Wagga Wagga, Australia: Centre for Information Studies.

Hopkins, D. M. (1999). *Issues in the education of school library media specialists* [Online]. Available: http://www.alalorg/congress/hopkins.html

Hopsicker, S. (1997). Moving every child ahead: The Big6 success strategy. *Multimedia Schools, 9*(3), 16–22.

Ishizuka, K., Minkel, W., & St. Lifer, E. (2002). 5 biggest challenges for 2002. *School Library Journal, 48*(1), 50–54.

Jacobson, F. F. (1997). Introduction. *Library Trends, 45*(4), 575–581.

Johnson, D. (1999). Implementing an information literacy curriculum: One district's story. *NASSP Bulletin, 83*(605), 53–61.

Jones e-global library. (2001). *Role of Librarians in the Digital Age* [Online]. Available: http://www.e-globallibrary.com

Kapitzke, C. (2001). Information literacy: The changing library. *Journal of Adolescent & Adult Literacy, 44*(5), 450–456.

Kranich, N. (2000). Why libraries are more popular than ever. *American Libraries, 32*(4), 5.

Kranich, N. (2001). A message from ALA President, Nancy Kranich, *American Libraries, 31*(11), 7.

Kuhlthau, C. C. (1989). An emerging theory of library instruction. *School Library Media Quarterly, 16*(1), 23–27.

Kysow, W., Shrive, A., Sihota, R., & Weichel, C. (2003). Constructing knowledge in the 21st century: A teacher-librarian's perspective. *Feliciter* [Online]. Available:http://www.cla.ca/feliciter/feliciter. com

Lance, K. C. (2001a). Proof of the power: Quality library media programs affect academic achievement. *Multimedia Schools, 8*(4), 14–20.

Langford, L. (2001). A building block towards the information literate school community. *Teacher Librarian, 28*(5), 18–21.

Lyman, P. (2000). Information literacy. *Liberal Education, 87*(1), 28–38.

McGovern, G. (2001). *Age of the Information Literate* [Online]. Available: http://wysiwyg://2http://www.clickz.com/design/site_design/article.php/837101

McGregor, J. H., & Streitenberger, D. C. (1998). Do scribes learn? Copying and information use. *SLMQ Online* [Electronic Version]. Available: http://www.ala.org/aasl/SLMQ

Minkel, W. (2002). Web of deceit. *School Library Journal, 48*(4), 50–54.

Mikalishen, W. (2001). The role of the teacher-librarian in the teaching of information literacy in the intermediate grades. *School Libraries in Canada, 21*(2), 20–22.

Mohn, P. G. (2000). The role of the librarian and technology. *Book Report, 20*(1), 32–33.

North High School Library. *Research Tips* [Online]. Available: http://www.csd99.k12.il.us/north/library

Online Computer Library Center, Inc. (2002, June). OCLC White paper on the information habits of college students [Online]. Available: http://www2.oclc.org/oclc/pdf/printondemand/information habits.pdf

Pappas, M. L. (2002). Teaching information skills: Appreciation. *School Library Media Activities Monthly, 18*(10), 25–27.

Pascale, R. (1990). *Managing on the edge: How the smartest companies use conflict to stay ahead.* New York: Simon & Schuster.

Pickard, P. W. (1993). Current research: The Instructional consultant role of the school library media specialist. *School Library Media Quarterly, 21*(2).

Pryor, S. (2001). Library media centers that learn: Applying the fifth discipline. *Book Report, 20*(2), 20–23.

Rafoth, M. A. (2001). *Inspiring independent learning: Successful classroom strategies.* Washington, DC: National Education Association Professional Library.

Rankin, V. (1996). Get smart. *School Library Journal, 42*(8), 148.

Reuters Guide to Good Information Strategy [Online]. Available: http://www.about.reuters.com/rbb/research/gis.html.

Riedling, A. M. (2000a). Great ideas for improving reference interviews. *Book Report, 19*(3), 28–29.

Riedling, A. M. (2000b). *Reference skills for the school library media specialist: Tools & tips.* Worthington, OH: Linworth Publishing.

Riedling, A. M. (2001a). In search of who we are: The school library media specialist in the 21st century. *Book Report, 20*(3), 28–32.

Riedling, A. M. (2001b). The question is the solution. *Book Report, 20*(1), 28–30.

Riedling, A. M. (2002). *Learning to learn: A guide to becoming information literate.* New York: Neal-Schuman.

Rockwell-Kincanon, J. (2001). Got Library?: Musings on marketing information literacy. *OLA Quarterly, 7*(2), 16–17.

Ryan, J., & Capra, S. (2001). *Information literacy toolkit.* Chicago: American Library Association.

Smith, J. B. (1987). Higher order thinking skills and nonprint media. *School Library Media Quarterly, 16*(1), 38–42.

Tanner, D. (1997). Standards, standards: High and low. *Educational Horizons, 75,* 115–120.

Thomas, N. P. (1991). *Information literacy and information skills instruction: Applying research to practice in the school media center.* Washington, DC: National Education Association.

Thompson, H. M., & Henley, S. A. (2000). *Fostering information literacy: Connecting national standards, Goals 2000, and the SCANS report.* Englewood, CO: Libraries Unlimited.

Todd, R. J. (1999). Transformational leadership and transformational learning: Information literacy and the World Wide Web. *NASSP Bulletin, 83*(605), 4–12.

Todd, R. J., & Kuhlthau, C. (2004). 13,000 kids can't be wrong. *School Library Journal 50*(2), 4–6.

Troutner, J. (2002). Information literacy activities and skills. *Teacher Librarian, 28*(5), 29.

Tschamler, A. (2002). Top secret: Collaborative efforts really do make a difference. *Library Talk, 15*(2), 14–17.

Turner, P. (1993). *Helping teachers teach* (2nd ed.). Englewood, CO: Libraries Unlimited.

Wolcott, L. L. (1994). Understanding how teachers plan: Strategies for successful instructional partnerships. *School Library Media Quarterly, 22*(3).

Wurman, R. (1989). *Information anxiety.* New York: Doubleday.

Yeager, E. A., & Silva, D. Y. (2002). Activities for strengthening the meaning of democracy for elementary school children. *Social Studies, 93*(1), 18–22.

Yucht, A. H. (1997). *FLIP IT! An information skills strategy for student researchers.* Worthington, OH: Linworth.

Index

About the Author

ANN MARLOW RIEDLING is Associate Professor at Saint Leo University, St. Petersburg. She has worked in the field of library science and information technology since 1974. Her previous books include *Reference Skills for the School Library Media Specialist: Tools and Tips*; *Catalog It! A Guide to Cataloging School Library Materials*; *Learning to Learn: A Guide to Becoming Information Literate*; *Helping Teachers Teach: A School Library Media Specialist's Role (3rd ed.)*, and a trade book, *How We Became Camels*.